PLEASE MAKE ME LOVE ME

PLEASE MAKE ME LOVE ME

a memoir

EMILY GINDLESPARGER

LIONCREST
PUBLISHING

Please Make Me Love Me

A Memoir

ISBN 978-1-5445-2957-8 *Hardcover*

      978-1-5445-2956-1 *Paperback*

      978-1-5445-2958-5 *Ebook*

The truth is you turned away from yourself,

and decided to go into the dark alone.

Now you are tangled up in others,

and have forgotten what you once knew,

and that's why everything you do

has some weird failure in it.

—KABIR

Contents

Author's Note ix

1. There's This Girl. 1

2. Emergency Cocktails 11

3. The Life I Tell Myself I Can't Have. 15

4. My Inner Wisdom Never Uses Her Words. 29

5. My Lifesaving Fuck Buddy. 35

6. We Say Yes to a Future We Can't Control 47

7. Flirting Is like Skydiving—Quick Thrill, Hard Landing . . . 51

8. The Ex Machina Drinking Game 61

9. The Worst Lie I Ever Told (Part 1) 71

10. Here Are All the Things I Wasn't Going to Tell You 79

11. The One-Dick Policy 91

12. Too Eager for Intimacy 97

13. Pick Me 105

14. Here's Why They Call It a Crush 113

15. When I'm Found, I Want to Hide 119

16. Mom, Meet My Secret Life 127

17. In Which I Make Rash Decisions. 135

18. Time Share 143

19. The Worst Lie I Ever Told (Part 2) 151

20. How a Secret Becomes a Bomb 161

21. Up in Smoke 169

22. Push and Pull 173

23. Stone Walls 181

24. Shitty Yoga 191

25. Basement Renovations. 199

26. Love Made Visible. 205

27. Holding Hands against the Ocean 213

28. Out in Public. 223

29. Reunited, Split Apart 227

30. The Talk, Take Two 237

31. The Millennial Family Portrait. 241

32. The First Ending. 245

33. Stray Wanders Home. 249

34. New Normal. 257

35. The Second Ending 261

36. The Third Ending. 275

37. Take Me Somewhere Beautiful. 281

Acknowledgments. 285

Author's Note

This book is nothing more than a reflection of my own personal truth and how I saw, felt, and experienced the world at a particular point in my life.

Specific scenes and dialogue are written as faithfully as I can remember them, but I have no doubt the people who went through these same moments walked away with entirely different understandings and their own truths of what happened.

To protect the privacy of others and the integrity of their own stories, I've changed names and identifying details in this book. Some people are composites of multiple relationships I had during this time in my life. Locations have been changed, and timelines were altered in some cases.

I worried for a long time about what I chose to write about and how the people who appear in these stories would feel about it. But then I realized I was trying to anticipate and manage other people's emotions instead of speaking my truth.

Which is my constant struggle, as you'll see from how this whole story plays out.

So, I've decided to share this story with you, not because it's "the truth" of these relationships, but because it's my own experience of an intense, imperfect time when I changed fundamentally, and I believe in sharing our stories so we can bring more humanity to the mess.

By the time you read this, no one in this book will be as they are described here. Not even me.

1

There's This Girl

"So, there's this girl I'm kind of interested in," Jordan said one morning.

I got an instant hot flash of panic. My eyes stayed glued to the student papers I'd graded the night before and was shoving in a binder to take to work. I wanted to look up at his face—to see if he was excited, or nervous, or apologetic, or bored with me—but my own face was suddenly made of stone, too heavy to lift.

The eggs Jordan was making sizzled and popped. He turned to the stove to stir them, and then he turned back to me. I kept packing my bag, mechanically, slowly.

Say something, I told myself. *The only way through this is to keep him talking so you don't have time to feel. All you have to do is run out the clock until you have to go to work.*

"Oh," I said. I couldn't think of anything else.

Jordan scooped eggs and vegetables out of the pan and onto two plates. He ground pepper over them and handed one plate to me. Breakfast looked beautiful. I wanted to cry. The smell of bacon and sweet potato made me feel sick. I stuck a fork in the hash anyway and made myself chew.

"Who is it?" I tried to knock the pitch of my voice down.

"Casey," Jordan said.

I knew Casey. Or I knew *of* her. I'd seen her at the dive bar we all liked to frequent. Casey had tons of funky, wild tattoos with great stories behind them, and she wore threadbare T-shirts that were messy and hot. She had dark hair and those short punk bangs that make your eye travel all over someone's face. She drank well whiskey and soda because the bartenders would pour strong if the drink was simple and she didn't give a fuck. She was friends with a couple of women who wore ruby-red lipstick and chipped black nail polish, and she always stood out because she was never dolled up.

I was not like Casey. I didn't have tattoos, especially not the kind on your thigh that people stare at when you sit with your knees apart. Hot summer nights at the dive bar, I wore sundresses and overpaid for blackberry mojitos from one bartender who smashed fresh fruit and mint in the bottom of the glass with a chunk of sugarcane and who always seemed a little proud when he handed the drink over.

I'd never talked to Casey because she always got to the bar late, and I always left early. Each time I got up to go at eight or nine, my friends would try to badger me into staying.

"She needs her sleep," Jordan would say. "In the morning she's teaching the youth of America."

He'd stay out a few more hours and crawl into bed at midnight or one. If I woke up as he shuffled the sheets, he would curl in close and hold me, and I would pull his arm over me to hold his hand against my chest. In the morning he would recap the half-drunk philosophical conversations I'd missed and list who'd shown up after I'd gone.

Casey. She was always there when I wasn't.

I hadn't sat down after Jordan handed me the plate. I was standing in the kitchen, holding the plate and a bite on my fork, and I realized:

He's had a whole life happening in those evenings without me. He could have a whole relationship with Casey that I know nothing about.

The breakfast I was trying to swallow became a lump in my throat. My panic ran a mile-a-minute monologue in my head.

She is so different from you—is that a good thing or a bad thing? Maybe it's a good thing, because it means he obviously still wants you, and he's just interested in what it would be like to make out with someone totally not like you. Or maybe it's a really bad thing, because he'll realize he picked the totally wrong type of person and he won't want you at all; how the fuck do you both get out of this crush alive?

"Do you…want to date her?" I choked out.

I ignored the biggest question that was bouncing around my brain: *Do you think she's sexier than me?*

"Yeah, I'm interested in that," Jordan said. My ears started to buzz, drowning out his words that followed. I only picked up snippets of what he said next.

"I don't feel like I need to do anything about my attraction, though. It's just that you and I have been having conversations about what it might be like to open our relationship in theory, and I think it's important to start talking about whether it's something we actually want to do."

I flicked my eyes up to his face for just a second. He looked unexpectedly relaxed, leaning back on the counter, but his plate sat untouched next to him. I turned my eyes back to my fork and tried to get more of my breakfast down.

"I need to get to work early this morning to finish prepping one of my lessons," I lied. I shoveled the last few bites of egg and kale into my mouth and downed a glass of water, hoping it would push everything down. "Let me think about it."

I put my plate in the dishwasher with a clatter, threw my bag over my shoulder, and picked up my keys. Everything was so loud. Jordan gently grabbed my arm as I reached for the door handle. I turned back, and he kissed me. I kept my lips tight in a peck.

"Have a good day teaching the youth of America," he said.

I smiled, said nothing, and closed the door.

. . .

Driving to work, I gripped the steering wheel so tightly my hands started to go numb. I felt a flood of rage and grief, like I was trying to process a breakup that hadn't happened yet.

Wasn't I enough?

Jordan and I had been together eight years by then, and in all that time we'd never talked about attractions we had to other people. We had, however, spent many road trips listening to Dan Savage spout off answers to people's sex and relationship questions on his advice podcast, *Savage Love.* We'd talked many times about whether either of us would ever want an open relationship. We'd landed on *maybe, maybe not, I don't know.*

I'd read *Sex at Dawn*, a book by Cacilda Jethá and Christopher Ryan on the biology behind human mating behavior, and I thought there was a compelling case for people not really being built for monogamy. I thought open relationships made logical sense, but now, faced with the idea of actually opening mine up, my emotions rebelled.

No one can be everything for a person, my logical brain reasoned.

My anxiety didn't give a shit about logic. I kept spinning. *What about me isn't working for Jordan anymore? If we don't open our relationship and Jordan never gets to explore his feelings, our relationship will wither with resentment and die.*

That's all definitely right, Radio K whispered. *There are no other possible explanations for Jordan telling you about another girl.*

Ah, Radio K. That's my pet name for the stream of snide, cynical, egotistical thoughts that run loops in my head. Ann Patchett once described how we have competing narratives, like radio stations, running through our brains, and she calls the destructive, malicious one "Radio K-Fuck." Radio K as a name for that voice stuck with me.

Once I named him, it was easier to hear him, which sucked because he became really loud, but also helped because I finally knew when he was speaking. Sometimes—only in fleeting moments— I could remember not to give him the last word.

Radio K took great joy in pinging the words around my brain: *there's a girl, a girl, a girl, a girl.*

By the time I got home, I'd spiraled so far into my anxiety that I couldn't bear to bring up the morning's conversation. Jordan didn't bring it up either; he seemed to be waiting for the moment I felt comfortable enough to talk. I didn't want to talk.

The next day, I said nothing to Jordan about Casey, but I was thinking about her all the time. She was a ghost that followed me around the kitchen and into the shower. I took forever to pick out clothes and get dressed. I measured all my wardrobe choices against what Casey would pick.

Be breezy, I thought. *If you get weepy or neurotic, he'll just want to leave.*

This was a classic projection, though I couldn't see it at the time. I didn't want to feel how I really felt. I didn't want to be around myself when I was falling apart.

So I convinced myself Jordan wouldn't be able to handle how I felt, and *he* was why I had to keep it together.

But I couldn't remember how to be the breezy, normal, light-hearted version of myself. *Do I usually hunch so much? I want to play with Jordan's hair, but I can't remember the last time I did that—will it seem like I'm overcompensating?*

When I got home from work, I insisted we put on a comedy because I didn't want to talk and I couldn't handle anything serious, but I couldn't remember what I would normally laugh at. All I wanted to do was cry in the bathtub and nuzzle into the center of Jordan's chest and not talk for a thousand years.

I crawled into bed early to read relationship self-help books. I bought Esther Perel's *Mating in Captivity* on my Kindle so Jordan couldn't see the cover of what I was reading. I wanted to make sense of Jordan's desire without talking to him about it. I was too afraid to hear more about what he wanted with Casey.

Jordan and I didn't have sex that week.

Oh, that's another thing—don't forget she'll probably be better at sex than you, Radio K whispered as I was trying to go to sleep. *I mean look at all those tattoos and how she uses her mouth when she talks, and your libido is like this nervous wild rabbit anyway, it never sticks around when you want it to, and once he realizes that he can be with someone who plays it cool and is down for sex anytime, he'll wonder what the hell he's doing with you...*

Fuck you, Radio K, I thought, but he just started his monologue all over again. He repeated it in my ear the following day as I tried to explain to my students the proper uses of a semicolon.

* * *

A night or two after Jordan said he was interested in Casey, I lay awake at two in the morning listening to Jordan snoring, feeling a creeping panic wrap its fingers around my rib cage.

I picked up my phone and googled *my boyfriend likes another woman what do I do.*

I felt stupid, looking to the internet, of all things, for advice on how I should feel. But I didn't like how I felt—angry, embarrassed, prudish, pathetic, desperate—and I wanted someone, even a faceless stranger, to tell me how I should feel instead.

I thought if someone could tell me the way out of this hellfire of self-doubt that was raging in my mind, I could just will myself to follow the directions. I could will myself to feel differently.

After several nights of thinking instead of sleeping, I finally burrowed my way down a rabbit hole that led to a revelation. I was upset about Jordan's attraction because I was terrified he would leave me. I thought for sure he would leave, because I could think of no reason he was with me except that I was in the right place at the right time, and maybe Casey had arrived in a better place at a better time.

Somehow, I'd constructed a story that Jordan's love was opportunistic. Did I really believe that the only reason Jordan loved me was because he didn't love someone else more?

Yes, yes I do.

I could think of nothing intrinsically worth loving about me. And worse, I thought the success of our relationship was the only way to prove I was loved, period.

I rely on Jordan's love to prove my worth, I realized.

This is not a sustainable plan.

Jordan's snores had given way to a deep-sleep kind of breathing: smooth long inhale, pause, quick exhale, like the weight of his lungs was too heavy.

I googled *how do I feel worthy.*

Everything I read seemed hollow and trite and riddled with affirmation practices. I hate affirmation practices. They make big important things feel fake.

I closed my eyes.

Here's an experiment, I thought. *Can I feel where my own love is?*

I could feel where I felt unloved, in the tightness of my chest, so heavy the last few days that every deep breath I took was a conscious and deliberate effort. I could feel shame in the heartburn that lightly seared a column from heart to throat. I could feel my fear in my hip flexors that kept me awake because my legs couldn't settle down.

Jesus, couldn't I feel my own love *somewhere*?

I asked this question over and over until I started to feel a little calm in small corners of my body. My elbows. The backs of my arms. The bones of my feet. Maybe one of my many ribs felt untouched by anxiety, I decided. Some parts of my body were opting out of feeling tortured. And because I'd been so sleepless, because I was so tired, I decided this was good enough to pass for love.

I decided those parts loved me.

I fell asleep. And when I woke up, things felt different, and they also didn't, which was depressing.

Some moments I felt better. In those moments I thought maybe it was a medium-sized risk, not a big one, to just see what it would feel like for us to date other people. We could always pull back, right? We could keep talking and designing what we wanted. Hope flashed at me like the scattered reflection on a pond after you've dropped a big rock in and caused all kinds of waves.

Then Radio K started up again.

You can't learn to love yourself, not really, and plenty of other people are just cruising through life without this kind of dread, and Jordan will find them and build a life with them and leave you, the basket case, to your own devices.

It seemed each time a little light was shed on my demons, they picked up their shovels and dug down somewhere deeper and darker.

2

Emergency Cocktails

By the end of the week, my nerves were so rattled I called an emergency happy hour with Zadie. I got to the bar patio early and ordered a sidecar and an espresso. The waitress looked at me sideways, then cracked a smile.

"I never thought to put the uppers and downers together like that," she said. "Sounds good, actually."

"It's what I do when I have no idea what to do," I replied.

I drank the sidecar fast and the espresso slow. The lemon tart of the cocktail opened my sinuses a little. The alcohol slowed my brain down enough that I could start to think one thought at a time. The sugar on the rim lingered in my mouth and made the coffee taste silky and Turkish.

I ordered another sidecar and opened my book while I waited for Zadie. I couldn't tell you what I was reading or whether I was really reading at all. Sometimes my brain goes too fast for words to make sense and my eyes just skid over the page like bald tires on black ice.

Zadie is one of those amazing friends who is so insanely busy you only get to see her once every two months for a four-hour catch up, but the conversation is so good it's as if you talked on the phone every day. She's a spitfire: five-foot-one with a short, severe haircut. She never wears uncomfortable clothing or shoes and has these billowy pants of printed cotton that almost look like a skirt with an artful twist in the middle. She has an opinion on everything, and she's the good kind of judgmental; she's discerning.

Zadie stomped up to the patio—sometimes she's so full of feisty energy, she can't help but stomp—and hugged me under the arms. She lifted me off the ground and gave a little bounce to crack my back. "Hi friend," she said as she set me back down. That's pretty much how Zadie greets her good friends, every time. I love her.

I started to cry right away. That's what happens when I'm around someone I know I can't bullshit.

Zadie sat down, took a sip of my cocktail, and listened patiently as I spilled the details about Jordan's crush and Casey's sexy nonchalance and how I suddenly felt like I was playacting my own life, so self-conscious about everything that I wished I could remember my own lines.

I got so deep in conversation so fast that the waitress wisely ignored us for at least forty minutes. Zadie finished my cocktail. I finished my espresso, which probably didn't affect my conversational speed for the better.

When I took a breath, Zadie asked, "What do *you* want?"

I paused for a long time, considering. "I don't even know," I said. And then I shut my mouth for a long time.

Zadie had gotten divorced the year before. The year before that, she had told her then-husband that she was interested in being with women. She didn't want to break up her marriage, but she didn't want to go her whole life without exploring her curiosity. She'd always known she was into women. She just hadn't known, until that last year of her marriage, how important it was to her.

When she talked about her desire to her then-husband, he totally shut down. He couldn't talk about it, let alone set up a plan that would allow Zadie a little experimentation. So Zadie gave him a year.

She waited patiently, periodically bringing the subject back up and letting him know it was still what she wanted. In private conversations between us girls, Zadie described in salacious detail the lesbian porn she was using to satisfy herself in the meantime.

On the patio, after she'd caught the eye of the waitress and ordered two more sidecars, she described again the last days of her marriage, when she finally decided to take the leap and break up because she wasn't getting what she needed. He'd never been able to even talk to her openly about her desire for women, much less sign off on her sleeping with someone else.

"I can't believe he wouldn't even talk to you about it," I blurted out. "He was not a good partner to you. He didn't even try."

As soon as the statement popped out of my mouth, I felt like I'd been smacked in the face. A headache bloomed behind my eyes.

"Oh my god," I said, "that's what I'm doing. I'm refusing to talk."

Zadie gave me a tender smile with her lips pursed just a little. She said nothing.

"I think I want to try," I said.

"Just have a conversation about it," Zadie said gently. "And think about what you want."

"I want Jordan to be happy."

Zadie shook her head. "Of course. But what do you want for *yourself?*"

I opened my mouth to answer, and then I closed it. *I want us to change and grow together. I want us to experiment with this one wild life. I want to feel secure in our relationship.* I looked around the patio at the other people dining; I looked across the street at the leaves hanging in the breeze. I couldn't think of anything that was just mine.

"I don't know what I want."

Zadie raised her eyebrows. "Good time to start thinking about it."

The panic I'd felt all week started to crack, and in the space below I felt something totally different: I felt relieved. Jordan had named his desire. He'd given himself permission to think about what might be possible for himself and our relationship.

I'd thought I would feel secure by never questioning whether we'd always be together—but maybe there was a deeper sense of security that could come from consciously choosing each other because we each know what we want.

Instead of assuming we were making each other happy, we could actually ask that question of ourselves and each other.

I downed the rest of my sidecar. My skin felt electric.

What do I want?

3

The Life I Tell Myself
I Can't Have

I rode my bicycle home in the dark with the wind and Zadie's question rushing in my ears.

What do I want?

My mind was contentedly blank. I felt buzzed and a little elated, pushing the pedals in rhythm, the streetlights swinging past as I rushed underneath them. I felt fast and steady and free.

Okay, my mind is clear. Now what do I want?

Still blank.

Do I have to answer now? Can't I just enjoy being in the moment?

No, I thought, *this is what happens every time I try to ask myself what I want. I think of the question, and then I distract myself from the question. I never come back to it.*

Seriously, what do I want?

I slowed down next to a tiny park where there was a bench right next to the bike path. I propped my bike against the bench and sat down. Then I felt restless, so I stood up.

I want to lock eyes with someone at a bar and watch them follow me around the room.

I want to dance without thinking about what people think and let my body move how it wants. I want someone to think how I move is beautiful, and I want them to tell me about it.

I want to swipe around on Tinder, just to get the sense of possibility: so many people who might want me, so many different women I could be to suit them.

I want to steal a drag off a stranger's cigarette, just to show I can be bold.

I want to be sexy. Playful. Mysterious. Coy. Direct. I'm tired of being reliable, predictable, sweet, good. I want to be mercurial, bitchy, effortlessly cool.

I want to be irresistible. To get validation for any version of myself I want to be.

I want to be chosen. To be picked out of a crowd. To be adored again by someone who doesn't know about the anxiety that claws my brain to shreds. Someone who doesn't notice how much I hesitate. Someone who can pull me out of myself.

I want to feel the energy of all the people I never let myself be.

As soon as this torrent of thoughts came through, I started to get cold. I shook my hands to warm them up. It was probably seventy degrees out.

I didn't want to want those things. The last time I had thoughts like this, I got so confused I blew up my relationship and moved clear across the country, here to Tucson. I didn't want my life to blow up again, so I got back on my bike and pedaled faster, hoping the speed would help me stop thinking.

* * *

I'd gone to college in Chicago, where I had a two-plus-year relationship with a man I really loved, Sam. When I graduated college, my best friend, Meg, and I decided to go out to the East Coast to be counselors at a high-adventure summer camp. It was a three-month gig and paid pennies, but since our housing and food would be covered, I'd still be able to save some money after paying my share of the rent on my Chicago apartment. After a fun summer, I'd come back to the city and get a real job. That was the plan.

Meg and I drove out to the camp together, and as soon as we got out of the car, she had a small flock of men gathering around, asking her to tell them about herself.

Meg was—and is—beautiful. She's one of those All-American-Girl types, with a heart-shaped face, honey-blond hair, and a prim little way of pursing her lips when she's concentrating. Everyone she met was in love with her. I was in love with her, though I didn't let myself think it. I was straight. I had a boyfriend. There was no reason to question any of it, no reason to suspect there was more of me to discover under the surface.

A lanky kid with a long pimpled face wanted to show Meg around the camp. I lagged behind them. I only half-listened to their conversation; I was watching Meg. She gave a short sparkly laugh to some joke he made, and she held her shoulders up in a quarter shrug. She was not into him. He asked me where I was from, and

I made a point of saying I lived in Chicago with my boyfriend. He promptly turned his attention back to Meg.

I repeated the line with all the other counselors, and it had the same effect. Not because I had a boyfriend, but because I was guarded in talking about myself. Soon I felt invisible. I watched Meg soak in the attention with such ease, and I felt jealous—both because she was in the spotlight and because I wasn't in her spotlight anymore.

The last night of our training week, one of the trainers pulled out a portable speaker and put on music: a folk band doing a cover of "Take Me Home, Country Roads," with a lively upright bass and a fiddle weaving through the vocal line. Several of the trainers got up and started dancing. One of them asked Meg to dance. I was sitting next to an annoying guy who'd piled rocks and sticks on the tabletop to build a model of the river we took the campers on. He was talking nonstop about the different water features and how they pushed the rafts around, and where exactly we needed to steer for a smooth ride. I wasn't listening—though I probably should have, because I went on to fail my raft guide test a few days later. Instead, I watched the dancers two-step, feeling a little jealous again.

The song switched to "Wagon Wheel," a tune I love. I excused myself from the table and wove my way into the middle of the knot of dancers. I was the only one dancing solo, but at least in the middle no one sitting at the tables could watch me. I felt sheepish by myself, so I closed my eyes.

When the chorus kicked up, a hand slid around the small of my back, and another hand caught my hand. I opened my eyes and there was Luke, one of the trainers, looking back at me. Luke swung me out in a spin and pulled me right back. He was a good dancer. He knew how to signal the next move by pressing my back with his fingertips.

It felt good to be chosen. To be seen. It felt good to be uninhibited. I danced one more song with Luke, and then the music switched to Radiohead and lost its barn dance appeal. I thanked Luke and went to bed early. No one tried to convince me to stay up.

The next morning, I wrote a letter to my boyfriend, Sam. I wrote about how much I liked waking up to the birds here, and how much I loved canoeing the river, and how tight sections of the caves were to squeeze through. I didn't write about dancing with Luke.

The rest of the summer, I wanted to be around Luke all the time. He was funny, and easygoing, and spontaneous. Whenever he concocted a new plan for some fun thing to do, I waited a few beats before getting up to follow him, hoping no one noticed I was always following him.

One night on our weekend off, a group of us older counselors snuck out to a bridge over the river to drink beers. One of the counselors brought the portable speaker and we played Tom Petty and Red Hot Chili Peppers while dangling our legs over the side.

Luke got a little buzzed, pulled off his shoes, and climbed up onto the steel girder a few feet above our heads. He started to walk the length of it out into the dark where we couldn't see him, and I called out to him to come back.

"You could slip and fall," I pleaded.

"Who cares?" he shouted back. "I don't have to follow your rules. You're not my girlfriend."

My face felt hot. I clenched my jaw. "I don't want to have to drag your ass out of here when you break an ankle or get hypothermia from falling in the river."

Luke didn't respond. He came back ten minutes later, shivering from the cold. He shoved his feet back in his shoes and took a swig of my beer.

I wrote more letters to Sam, one per week. I wrote about how I helped campers get over their fear of heights or their fear of tight spaces. Sam never wrote back.

He's busy, I thought.

He doesn't want to hear this, Radio K snickered.

I wrote about how ecstatic I was to be in the mountains, playing outdoors every day. How I loved waking up with a cold face every morning and knowing where to find jewelweed when a camper got into poison ivy. I didn't want to go back to Chicago, but I didn't write that.

When camp ended, some of the counselors stayed behind for one more week to have a few last adventures on the river. We stayed at a campground where the host had a little cabin he let us all pile into, and we slept on the floor, packed together so tightly that when someone got up to pee, they had to carefully plot their course across the room to avoid getting tangled up in people's legs. I laid my sleeping bag out next to Luke's. The last night, as everyone was falling asleep, Luke slid his hand over to my sleeping bag. I turned toward him, and he kissed me.

My whole body flooded with adrenaline. *This is wrong,* I thought, but the wrongness of it made all my senses feel heightened. Every crinkle of my sleeping bag suddenly sounded so loud. I wanted to press as much of my body against his as possible.

After several seconds, Luke finally pulled back and took a breath. "I guess I'm a homewrecker now," he whispered, so quietly no one else could hear.

The air suddenly felt thick with everyone else's breathing. I felt like I needed to throw up. I sat up and shimmied out of my sleeping bag, then picked up my pillow and my bag and stepped quietly over probably-not-sleeping bodies to get outside and get fresh air.

Just as I was shutting the door, Luke was there, slipping out behind me. It was a full moon, and out here I could see his face. My heart was pounding, and I felt thrilled and nauseated at the same time. Luke looked relaxed, like always, with a slight smile playing on his lips.

"Want to sleep out here?" he asked.

I nodded and crawled into my sleeping bag. A voice in my head yelled, *What do you want to do here?*

Part of me answered, *I don't want to go back to Chicago.*

Radio K said, *That's the wrong answer. You have to go back to Chicago. It's the responsible thing to do, and you are oh-so-responsible, aren't you?*

My cheeks burned and my mind went blank. I didn't have another answer.

I swallowed to try to clear the heartburn that had risen up my throat. And then I turned to Luke and kissed him. I felt so desperate to hold on to the magic of the silvery moonlight in the grass, the high hum of the crickets, the fireflies and glow worms making constellations across the field. I knew I wasn't in love with Luke, but I was in love with this place, in love with the river and the cliffs above it and the friends I'd made who were ready to get in a truck and do something new at the drop of a hat.

I knew as soon as we all left the next day, I'd be going back to trains and bus schedules, the smell of asphalt and garbage, and skyscrapers that only let in the daylight for a few hours around high noon each day. *And you'll be going back to Sam. You love Sam.*

I kissed Luke, hoping I could convince myself to find a way out of my future and back here to the river. I knew it was ludicrous. And when Luke's hands crept further around the zipper of my sleeping bag, I stopped him.

"I don't want to go any further. We're all leaving tomorrow, and I'm going back to Sam. I don't want to cross a line I can't come back from."

Haven't you already? Radio K asked.

Behind his judgment, a smaller, gentler voice surfaced. *You know what you want, and you are choosing to go back to what you don't want. The first line you are crossing is a line within yourself. Every decision after that one takes you further away from yourself.*

"Okay," Luke said. He left his hand resting on my waist. I twisted around to lie flat on my back. I couldn't think of what to say, so I pointed out Cassiopeia in the stars above us and tried to tell Luke as much as I could remember about the myth that put her up there, chained to her chair. Luke didn't say anything else.

No-see-ums came out and started biting my neck and arms like crazy, so I curled into my sleeping bag and tugged the hood strings tight around my face to keep them out. I fell asleep like that, and by the time I woke up in the morning most everyone was awake and bustling around, packing up to leave.

When I hugged Luke goodbye, I copied the hugs I'd given other friends. I willed myself not to make this hug different.

* * *

I was excited to see Sam when I got back to Chicago. I didn't tell him there was a trainer named Luke there or that I'd kissed him. I was starting a new chapter of my adult life, and I thought maybe I could do it without looking back.

Things started to go sour in the winter, when it got so cold walking around the city that I just wanted to scream, and sometimes did, because people who live in big cities don't give a fuck. The city that had felt so magical when I was in school and constantly surrounded by harebrained creative people suddenly turned lackluster overnight.

Train brakes were constantly screeching everywhere I went. Lights were always on. People were always talking. Or staring. Or swaying on the subway, hanging on to the poles and trying to pretend no one around them existed. It took more than three hours to drive to the nearest nature preserve, which was sandwiched between a highway and a railroad and sounded like an urban white noise machine.

Everything started to grate my nerves. I was angry all the time. I hung on to a steady undertone of rage that I never really let myself feel because I told myself it didn't make sense. If I were to admit I hated my life, then I'd have to change it.

This, I now know, is depression. I didn't like how I felt, so I tried to stop feeling.

I was writing and submitting my work to journals and magazines, but no one seemed to want it. As rejection letters rolled in, I pinned them up on the wall of my tiny writing nook under the stairs. For a while they motivated me—evidence that I wasn't giving up. But when they really started to pile up, I pulled them down and put them in a thick manila envelope that I shoved in a drawer.

With no money coming in from my writing, I took a job at Trader Joe's. At least twice a week we'd run out of the precooked microwavable frozen brown rice. For some goddamn reason, the weeknight menu of every affluent Lakeshore family depended on frozen precooked brown rice, so twice a week some disgruntled middle-aged customer would gripe at me about it.

You don't get to have everything you want, I wanted to scream at them. Every time it happened, I locked myself in the dairy refrigerator and kicked in all the empty cardboard boxes. Then I gathered up all the smashed boxes from the floor and took them to the baler.

Sam had no idea what to do with me. I cried all the time and felt too afraid to explain why. I begged him to ride bikes with me to Lake Michigan in the dead of winter. I wanted to walk down the block to the thrift store to shop all the hand-me-down designer clothes with their signature mildewed-moldy-sweat smell, drenched in five different scents of laundry detergent. Sam declined these tempting suggestions.

I'd spend twenty minutes of my thirty-minute lunch break walking to and from my apartment, where Sam would be engrossed in a video game with our roommates. No one would look up. I'd eat a slice of cheese and walk the ten minutes back. I wanted Sam to look up. I wanted to kick the TV in and pretend it was an accident.

I cried every day and wore away a couple of months like that. I called my friends from camp, including Luke, and I felt better when I talked to them.

Sometimes I initiated sex with Sam when I didn't actually want to have it. The dull, dragging edge of depression was too much on my skin, and I wanted some other sensation. But I couldn't get into sex with him anymore. I remember looking at the mirror in our bedroom while we were having sex and thinking, *I look awkward and ugly.* I remember thinking, *I don't want to do this anymore.*

I didn't even know what "it" was—living in Chicago? Being with this man? Working at Trader Joe's? Beating myself up? Whatever "it" was, I kept doing it.

. . .

"It" finally became too much, and I called my brother in Arizona. It was seventy degrees and sunny in December in Tucson. I asked if I could come stay with him for a couple of months.

I only had enough money to buy the gas to get me there, but I figured I could get a job and it wouldn't take long to save enough money to drive back. My brother said yes.

I quit my job at Trader Joe's. They only allowed two weeks' vacation time, and I didn't know when I'd be back. I packed up my car, wedging my kayak into the back, somehow making it fit on the diagonal. There was no whitewater in all of southern Arizona, but I wanted the boat with me anyway. It was a token of the kinds of adventures I wanted to bring into my life from then on.

I didn't break up with Sam. He gave me the warmest hug the day I left.

"I think this will be a good reset," I told him as I pulled away. "I think I'll know what to do when I get back." I thought I'd come back in a better season, find a better job, find a better attitude. Simple.

He held on to my hands. "You're the most amazing person," he said. He looked me straight in the eye. I wanted to look away, but his face was so gentle and sincere that I couldn't. "You're the coolest person I know. Remember that."

I felt like such shit that I couldn't imagine why he said that. I was too overwhelmed and sad to ask.

* * *

I saw two sunrises through the car windshield and cried each time, but this crying felt different. It started to feel kind of good. Release instead of terror.

In Chicago I'd cried because I didn't want what was coming next. Another night shift at work where customers kept asking for things they felt they deserved but that we didn't have. Another lonely walk in the fucking freezing cold to come home and be greeted by no one. Sleeping through the daylight hours and missing the sun.

On the drive, I could feel the air tick a few degrees warmer with every mile. I cried because everything seemed beautiful. A dark thunderhead in Oklahoma that teased the horizon but never blocked out the sun. A blank highway in New Mexico where I stopped and laid on the hood of my car to see billions of stars. White sand dunes that looked like snow but never melted. I stopped and walked around, curious how long it would take the wind to erase my footprints and leave a clean slate again. Hours? Weeks?

Crossing into the border of Arizona, I got a little flicker of knowing. *It feels good to be on my own.*

But then Radio K whispered, *You're not in your right mind right now. You're acting crazy. Who just packs up and leaves a good man?*

I felt the familiar mix of dread and self-doubt creep into my chest as I stopped for gas. I tried to think of some retort. *Who can stay frozen in a cold place for so long?*

At that thought, a big heaving sob came through me all at once and I cried so hard my contact fell out. It was a rigid contact. They cost over a hundred dollars per eye. I lost it somewhere in the oil stains on the pavement. Then I cried harder because I knew I couldn't afford to replace it.

What do you want?

I wanted to stay in Tucson already, and I wasn't even there yet. I wanted to feel movement and light again. I knew Sam loved me, and I wanted to be able to feel it, but everything in Chicago felt dull and blunted and gray.

Your problem, Radio K hissed, *is that you want things you can't have.*

Sunset was painting the mountains in the distance purple and orange. The sky was so big I took bigger breaths to take in more of it.

Can't I?

4

My Inner Wisdom
Never Uses Her Words

When I ask myself what I want, lots of voices chime in. There's a small, nervous one that asks me whether I've thought about *this* and *this* and *this* and *this*. There's a gruff one that sometimes calls me a dipshit. There's a sweet woman's voice that often tricks me by saying, *I love you—but honey, are you sure?* They all argue constantly. Radio K sits off to the side, narrating the proceedings and making fun of me.

How am I supposed to find a single source of truth in all that?

My inner guidance doesn't answer questions. Instead, she sends me lurches of emotion that feel like a fifteen-year-old trying to jimmy a stick shift into first gear. Out of nowhere—*bam*—a flood of tears, a flush of panic, a burst of laughter no one really gets. My emotions used to not make sense to me, so I didn't listen to her.

In those depressing months in Chicago, she kept sending me a dream. It was very short. I was walking along a familiar street. It was daytime, but the skyscrapers were blocking the light on both sides like usual. A strange man walked up to me. He was tall, slightly attractive, with dirty blond hair. When I got within reach, he grabbed me and laid me down in the middle of the street. He started to tear at my clothes.

At first, I thought *yes—aggression can be so sexy sometimes, maybe I should just give into this*—but as soon as he'd torn my jeans down to my knees, I thought *no no no no no—this is...* There was literally no word I could think of for how terrifying and hideous and awful this is.

Suddenly the street, which had been entirely empty, was full of people. They surrounded me and watched what was happening to me, and no one said a word. I couldn't speak. It was one of those dream-tricks where you can feel in your throat and neck and temples how hard you're screaming, but nothing comes out.

The dream was not a recreation of anything I could pinpoint in my waking life. Yet this dream came up a couple of times a month. Some nights I didn't want to go to sleep, afraid the dream would come back.

More than a decade later, the memory of that dream came back to me while I was lying on a table, with an energy worker holding my head in her hands. At first my mind was blank while we did breathwork together.

Then my hands and mouth started to cramp so much that I couldn't move them.

I tried to tell Angela, the energy worker, what was happening to me, but my tongue was thick and frozen, and my cheeks were pulled tight. I couldn't get my muscles to shape the words.

Her dog jumped up and laid over me on the table. He was a huge fluffy lion of a dog who must have weighed a hundred pounds. Angela had introduced me to him at the beginning of the session. "He sometimes helps me with the work," she'd said.

That night, he was holding me down to earth, making sure I didn't dissolve. Slowly I started to calm down.

When I could move my mouth again, the first thing I told Angela about was this dream that had come to me a decade earlier. I don't know why; it just popped into my head. Intensity matching intensity.

"I'll let you in on a little secret," Angela said. "All the people in your dreams are you. In what ways have you not listened to yourself? When have you betrayed yourself?"

I had no answer for her. My mind went blank. Not because I couldn't think of anything, but because I couldn't snatch one thought out of the tornado of shame-guilt-rage-panic that swirled thoughtlessly in my head at the question.

Betrayed yourself? Radio K started up. *Let's start with when you betrayed other people. You get no sympathy. You betrayed Sam when you kissed Luke. You betrayed Luke when you kissed Luke. You left Chicago like a coward and betrayed Sam again by pretending you would come back.*

Radio K also had a long list of betrayals I'd perpetrated in the years since. *Over time, you end up betraying everyone.*

The lion of a dog was still lying across my body, holding me down. I felt a rush of gratitude to him for somehow knowing I needed support, for jumping up to be with me, for staying with me as I calmed down. My tears streamed down into my hair.

When have I left my own side?

It was a gentler version of the same question, a little easier to answer. I thought of the times I didn't want to have sex with Sam but had it anyway so Sam wouldn't know I was depressed. I thought of times I'd laughed nervously at some awful misogynistic joke because I wanted men to like me. All the feelings I'd shoved away because they were inconvenient or disruptive. All the feelings I'd shoved away because they might upset people I loved. I'd promised Sam I would come back to Chicago because I thought I was willing to trade my own mental health to be with him.

I betrayed myself constantly in the effort to be liked, to keep the peace, to control my inner world from spilling out. Because I had no qualms about betraying myself, I betrayed others just as easily.

Many years later, I realized when I feel most ashamed of myself, I go blank. It's a defense mechanism. *How could I be responsible for anything when I don't even know what I think or feel?* But the inverse becomes equally destructive. *How can I make the right decisions for myself if I don't know how I feel?*

What I'm trying to say is that I did some crazy things in my desperate attempts to not be "crazy" and emotional. *Don't leave a good man when you're depressed,* I thought in those final months in Chicago. *You're not in your right mind.* I stayed stuck.

All those years later, on Angela's table, I realized that in that terrible dream I was the woman lying in the street, and I was the man standing over her. I felt vulnerable and scared, and I overpowered those parts of myself. Like the crowd in the street, I silently watched myself deny my own reality. I said nothing.

I called my mother and cried on the phone, and when she asked what was going on, I just kept saying, "I don't know."

Since then, I've gotten slightly more familiar with the image-language of my inner wisdom. Once I asked what I should do about another stuck point in my life, and my inner wisdom sent me a vision of a woman with a fox head. The fox-woman stood in front of a bonfire, and she handed me a sparkler.

I asked her, *What the hell am I supposed to do with this?*

She just gave me a sly-fox smile. *Set fire to some things in here.*

Another time, she had me dive into a cenote—an underwater cave that was somehow filled with turquoise light. I came back up with an armful of black pearls the size of bowling balls.

When I wondered, *What do I do with these?* the only answer that came to me was, *Who knows, but damn, aren't they beautiful? Take time to really look at them.*

Sometimes I ask her what to do about all the spinning thoughts in my head and she just picks dandelions and blows them into the wind.

5

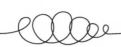

My Lifesaving
Fuck Buddy

In Tucson I took a job at an outdoor-gear shop, where all my coworkers were hikers and rock climbers. Some came to Tucson to pursue master's degrees at the university; some landed there for the world-class rock climbing. One of the few people who'd actually been born and raised in Tucson was a tall, lithe guy with a long neck and almost-shoulder-length red hair. He cracked easy jokes and knew how to tease people without embarrassing them. He sang goofy parody songs at work that were just shy of annoying and usually perked everyone up, even as they shook their heads. He gave frequent high fives.

The first time we clapped hands, I blushed and beelined to a rack of clothes that needed straightening. My third day at work, I needed to ask him a question, and I got so nervous that I forgot his name and called him Logan. Everyone noticed. "His name is *Jordan*," someone corrected me.

Someone posted a note in the backroom by the employee lockers saying that they were throwing a party at their house that Friday. I rode my bike the five miles from work back to my brother's place to fix a bite to eat before the party, and as soon as I walked in the door, I realized I'd forgotten to write down the address. I didn't have anyone's phone number.

My piece-of-shit car had broken down shortly after I'd gotten into town, so I jumped back on my bike and sprinted the five miles back to work. I just barely squeaked past the manager as he was locking up, wrote down the address on my hand, and rode ten more miles across town to the party.

I was sweating and panting by the time I arrived. A block away from the house, I got off my bike and walked, trying to regain my composure as Radio K called me ridiculous and desperate inside my head.

I opened the door to find three coworkers sitting on the couch, chatting, with beers in their hands, while two more were climbing around the room trying not to touch the floor. One of the guys from the shop, Nate, was on his tiptoes on the edge of the baseboard, holding the window frame for balance. Another guy, Jack, was stretched like a starfish across the corner of the room, toes on the baseboards, with his hands pressed against the adjacent walls. And at the threshold of the kitchen, there was Jordan, wrapped around the doorway like a koala. "The floor is lava!" he cried out as I stepped through the door.

These are my people, I thought.

Later, when the floor became a floor again so Nate could show Jack a balance trick, I watched Jordan cross the room and go out to talk to people on the front porch. I waited a beat so it wouldn't be too obvious, and then I followed. Everyone was in puffies and hats, and Jordan looked at me in my jean jacket and sandals.

"Aren't you cold?" he asked.

I shook my head. "I'm just starting to thaw."

A middle-aged man walked down the street alone, and when he saw all of us gathered on the bright porch, he came up the walkway toward the house. He was wearing just a T-shirt, and he rubbed his arms as he talked.

"Excuse me," he said. "I'm not from here; I just came to town to get my daughter, but I only had enough money for my Greyhound ticket and our bus tickets back. I've got my daughter now, but it's a cold night and we have nowhere to stay. I got robbed as soon as I got into town, and they took my wallet and all my cash. I can't afford a hotel room. Y'all got any money you might be able to spare to help me and my girl get a place to stay?"

I'd become jaded to stories like this. On my daily walk across the Chicago River to the train station, there was always a woman who sat on a piece of cardboard on one side of the bridge, shouting, "Got any change? I got no shoes. Got any change so I can buy shoes?" When I walked to the other side of the bridge, I would see a pair of women's size nines tucked into a little alcove.

I knew it was just a tactic, and the woman really did need money, even if she also had shoes. But I stopped trusting that the stories anyone told strangers were true.

My new friends stood up on the porch and started digging in their pockets for bills to hand the guy. I pursed my lips and leaned against the wall.

Jordan pulled off his coat, a canvas jacket with faux shearling lining, and held it over the railing for the man. "Stay warm out there," he said, and the man unfolded his arms and reached for the jacket. "God bless you," he said, with genuine relief in his voice. "God bless; thank you."

My heart softened just a little. I still thought Jordan and the others had been had. But in that interaction was a kind of care that I hadn't given or received in those depressed months in Chicago. I wanted to care again, and trust again. I thought Jordan could teach me.

• • •

My first day off, Jordan took me climbing. We took the scenic highway into the mountains, parked in front of a steep, craggy ridge, and picked our way carefully up the slope to the cliffs a few hundred feet above the highway. As we unpacked our gear, Jordan showed me the lines we were going to climb and pointed out the different features. He explained what he planned to do at each stage of the climb and described how he was going to anchor at the top of the first pitch and belay me from there. I'd never climbed on traditional gear before, and he showed me all the pieces and how they worked.

He moved gracefully and deliberately, dancing up the rock. In no time, he shouted down to me that he'd reached the top and it was my turn. The rock was cold. I started to shiver, but I also felt very awake. I tried to make my movements smooth like Jordan's had been. I took slow breaths, listening to the hiss of each exhale.

The canyon was so narrow that we didn't see the storm clouds roll in until they were right on top of us. It started snowing. I laughed and turned my face up to feel the cold snowflakes on my eyelids. It was the first time in a long time that I'd been out in the cold and not felt frozen.

By the time I reached the top, the snow had turned to hail. I was beaming. Jordan seemed surprised when he saw the joy on my face. He told me I was a badass.

Later that week, Jordan asked if I wanted to go on a night hike after our shift. We drove in his car out to the trailhead, and when we got out, all the rocks were lit up silver by the moon. Jordan brought a headlamp, but I told him not to turn it on.

The moon was so bright, we could see our shadows. In front of us, the mountain was cast in black and white, and behind us the city was splayed out in amber lights. I tripped a few times on the rocks.

"Let me turn on the light," Jordan said. "I don't want you to sprain an ankle out here."

"It would be worth it for how beautiful it is out here in the dark," I said.

At the end of our hike, Jordan gave me a hug before we got back in his car. We both held on for a long time. He was a full foot taller than me, and I could feel his face against the side of my head. He shifted his face a little, and I wondered if he was thinking about kissing me. I didn't look up. I knew I'd want to kiss him back.

I still hadn't broken up with Sam. I hadn't told any of my new Tucson friends about him. Standing in the trailhead parking lot in a hug that was lasting too long, I knew it was time to end it with Sam. I no longer felt I was crazy for leaving Chicago. I felt steadier here among mountains. I didn't want to go back, and Sam didn't want to move. It was time to let go.

. . .

Two weeks later, I was driving back across the country—this time with my brother and sister-in-law and their two large dogs—to see my parents for Christmas. Stuck in the back under the weight of a Weimaraner, with the Pointer breathing sticky dog-food breath in my face, I tried to make myself sleep as much as possible. My mind was spinning. My parents only lived six hours away from Chicago, an easy train ride to Sam, but I realized I didn't want to see him. I cried silently in the back seat while my brother blared Bruce Springsteen in the front.

We stopped at a rest stop on the western border of Oklahoma, and my brother and sister-in-law took the dogs for a walk. I called Sam. The wind whipped my hair, and I wondered if he'd be able to hear me clearly. I didn't give much preamble. I tried to stumble through my thoughts quickly so I wouldn't chicken out.

"We're getting back to Illinois in about ten hours, and…I don't want to come up to Chicago while I'm back. I…need to break up."

Sam was quiet for a few beats. "I don't want it to end like this. I need to see you."

I shook my head, phone pressed to my ear. "It's Christmas. I think we should spend time with our families."

"I'll drive down to see you," Sam said.

"I don't want you to do that." I could feel my throat closing up.

"I need to do this," Sam said.

I paused for a long time. In the distance I could see my brother and sister-in-law turning around from the walk with the dogs, heading back to the car. "Okay."

"Where are you?"

"Nowhere, Oklahoma. At a rest stop. We're about to get back on the road." I was anxious for the conversation to be over.

"Drive safe," Sam said. "I'll head down to you tomorrow."

"Okay." I hung up. We all piled back into the car, and I took my seat, squashed between the dogs. I didn't say anything to my brother or sister-in-law. I didn't want to talk.

* * *

Sam arrived at my parents' house around ten at night on Christmas Eve. I took him up to my childhood bedroom to talk. By three in the morning, we were worn out and not making sense to each other anymore. I felt numb and hot and dizzy, and all I could say to him was that I still didn't know what was wrong, but I needed it to be over.

He said he understood. I don't think he meant he understood me; I think he understood nothing was going to change.

We slept for two hours, and he woke up before dawn and drove back to Chicago. Christmas morning, I told my family Sam had already come and gone, and the relationship was over. I tried not to dampen the mood. I made cookies with my mom and hummed along to the music so I wouldn't have to talk and maybe she would think I was okay.

By dinner, my brother and I had made a plan to drive up to my Chicago apartment and move everything out. I told him I didn't want to take away from time with family to deal with it, but he shook his head.

"Let me help you. You'll feel better after you rip off the Band-Aid," he said.

Sam was away at his parents' house for the holidays. I walked through our apartment, packing up the few things I'd left behind when I'd filled my car a month ago. There were so many things we owned together, and I wasn't sure what to take. The Harry Potter books we'd bought one at a time from thrift stores. The record player. The cat. I left them all.

On the way back, my brother played *The Flying Cup Club* on the stereo, and I looked out my side window. I could cry in private that way as long as my shoulders didn't shake too much.

That night, Jordan called. I liked the sound of his voice, gentle and upbeat. "Did you get any loot for Christmas?"

I laughed. *More than I bargained for,* I thought. But I described the hiking pack my mom had given me, grateful to have a moment of feeling like a kid, like presents were still an important part of Christmas.

* * *

A week or so after I got back to Tucson, Jordan and I went on a nighttime community bike ride together. I liked getting lost in the swarm of forty bikes, weaving through neighborhood streets. One rider towed a little trailer with speakers blaring music.

Sometimes we rode next to the music, taking our hands off the handlebars and waving our arms in the air; sometimes we zipped up to the front, away from the music, so we could talk. It felt good to move. I felt free.

After the ride, I invited Jordan back to my brother's house, where I was still staying. The lights were off inside the house; my brother and sister-in-law were asleep. I led Jordan into the backyard, hopped up on the brick grill, and pulled him in to kiss me. He slipped my knit hat off and slid his fingers through my hair.

I wasn't thinking about the cat or the man I'd left in Chicago. I felt the cold brick under my ass, Jordan's cool hands slipping inside my jacket, the warmth of his bottom lip in my mouth.

Silently, I led him through the dark house, into the guest room I'd taken over. Jordan didn't give away whether he noticed that the bed we sank down onto was an air mattress. I hoped it wouldn't leak. I'd already woken up twice in the night to find myself on the floor, the mattress totally deflated, and groggily patched the leaks with bike tube patches. But in this moment, I wasn't thinking about how pathetic I was. I pulled off my shirt thinking about how good his hands would feel on me.

"I just got out of a long-term relationship and I'm not looking for anything serious," I said in a rushed whisper.

"Okay," he whispered back.

We didn't say anything else about our relationship or what we planned to do. I put my hand over my mouth to remind myself not to moan in my brother's house. Jordan left well after midnight.

In the morning, my brother handed me my knit hat with a puzzled look on his face. "I found this outside," he said.

"Oh, Jordan came over for a bit and we chatted in the yard," I said. Blushing, I took the hat, shoved it in my bag, and left for work. Jordan was on the same shift. We snuck into one of the back warehousing tunnels and made out against the stacks of shoes.

* * *

A week or so later, my brother and I went out for a bike ride. We were getting geared up at the car when my phone rang. It was Sam. I picked up and said hello, but Sam didn't say hello back.

"Who is Luke?"

A wave of icy-cold guilt crashed over me. I'd never told Sam about Luke. I thought I could just leave Luke back at camp and in the past. *How had Sam found out about him? What had he found out about him?*

"What are you talking about?" was all I could choke out. I knew it was evasive, but I couldn't think of any other way to start this conversation.

"Our joint phone bill was higher last month. So I went through it. You made lots of calls to someone named Luke. Who is he?"

"He's a friend from camp," I said. "I made lots of calls to all my friends at camp." I knew, though, that I'd called Luke more times than any of the others. I'd felt lonely and deadened inside, and his voice was always vibrant and alive. The last time I'd called him was on my drive out to Tucson.

"Are you seeing him?" Sam demanded.

"No."

"I don't buy that."

"He's a friend. He lives clear across the country. And it's not your business anymore, anyway." I looked sideways at my brother, who was busying himself with lubing the chain on his bike.

I wanted to throw my phone against a rock. I wanted to throw up, if only to get this burning-acid feeling out of the pit of my stomach. I wanted to erase the last messy year of my life.

You kissed Luke, Radio K piped up, *which means you deserve to feel this awful. And you've jumped straight into sleeping with Jordan before you've even atoned for the sins of your last relationship. You should be ashamed of yourself.*

"Are the overages on the bill from my phone calls?" I asked Sam, my hand shaking the phone against my ear.

"No, the overage turned out to be from something else on my phone."

"Okay. I have to go," I said, and hung up. Hot tears rolled down as I tossed my phone into the front seat of the car. I was shaking.

I moved in slow motion as I clipped my helmet and pulled my gloves on.

"Do you want to do this?" my brother asked. I nodded.

I want to scream.

I want to be in the mountains.

I want to push myself hard so I remember I can be strong even when I feel like shit.

"You'll feel better after you move," he said.

I pushed into the pedals so hard that my thighs burned. My brother rode fast, and I tried to grab his tail, so I tore down a stony hillside, my wheels pummeling the rocks. I kept repeating the lesson my brother had told me: *a rolling wheel is a steady wheel.*

My brother was right. Trying to keep up with him, I was frustrated and panting, but I wasn't thinking about Sam. My thighs burned and I felt better.

I didn't see the boulder until my front wheel stopped dead against it. I catapulted past the handlebars and landed against a barrel cactus. The needles slashed lines across my shin, and the impact ground dust and pebbles into my torn-up knee.

Looking at it, I could tell it should hurt. It didn't.

Blood streamed into my sock, and I didn't bother to wipe it away. I was grateful to be numb.

Numbness is one way to be free, Radio K whispered. *You don't have to feel your depression, your anxiety, your guilt. You can feel nothing.*

Because I couldn't imagine a middle ground between feeling like shit and feeling nothing, I believed him.

On the way home, my brother and I stopped at the grocery store for a few things. Everyone in the store stared at my bloody leg. They looked astonished. Or disgusted. I probably shouldn't have walked around like that in a place that sold food.

But I reveled in their shocked faces. I smiled and said hi. *Look at that girl,* I imagined them thinking. *She looks really hurt but she seems happy. She must be a badass.*

I bet she's the kind of girl who does whatever she wants.

6

We Say Yes to a Future
We Can't Control

"I'm ready to give it a shot," I told Jordan. We were standing in the kitchen. I looked at his hand holding the counter instead of looking.him in the eye. He has knobby knuckles. I thought about how it's a miracle humans survive with veins tracing so close under the skin.

I want to trust we're strong enough to experiment.

"Give what a shot?" Jordan asked.

"You dating Casey. I'm ready for us to try an open relationship."

"Oh." He seemed surprised, which I didn't quite get. *Hasn't he been obsessing over this question for the last week, just like I have?* "Okay, yeah. Um—should we set up some ground rules?"

"I'm not sure I want to know much of anything," I said. "I think it's good to know when you want to date someone, and who it is, but I don't think I want to know what happens on dates or anything."

"Okay." He thought for a moment, reached for a mug to make his tea. "I think if you start dating someone, I'll want to know all the details. I'll want to talk about it, to know how you're feeling."

"I think I can do that," I said.

Famous last words, Radio K sniped. Radio K always recognizes when I say something vague to cover when I'm not ready to talk about some friction I feel. I didn't know if I was going to date anyone. *But you want to experiment. Who knows who you might become when you let yourself be anyone? Will you be willing to let people in then?*

"So, I want you to feel free to date Casey," I cut across Radio K. "I guess just let me know if you set up a date with her."

"Okay," Jordan said, and I went to take a shower while he drank his tea.

A couple of weeks later, Jordan told me he was going to meet Casey at an Italian restaurant for pizza, on a night I was going to be teaching a yoga class. I told him that would be okay. Then he told me I was welcome to drop by before class if I wanted.

I felt a little flare of anger. *I don't want to sit there comparing myself with Casey while the food gets cold.*

Then anxiety. *I don't want you to leave me for her.*

Then denial. *I don't want to back out of our open relationship before we've even tried it. I don't back out on things just because I'm scared.*

"Sure," I said.

I rode my scooter to the pizza place. I got there a little late because my scooter was from the eighties and didn't have a gas gauge, so I ran out of gas on the way there and had to stop to fill up. When I walked in, Jordan and Casey were mid-conversation over a zucchini-noodle antipasto. I hoped my yoga leggings made me look fit and my jacket and helmet made me look cool. Casey was underdressed and confident in a tissue-thin black tank and cutoff shorts.

I sat down, and they immediately put a plate in front of me and spooned a portion of the zucchini noodles for me to eat. Jordan pushed his glass of wine over to me. "I know you've only got a little bit; drink up. I'll order myself another glass."

Casey said she was glad I could meet them, and I made sure to chew and swallow my bite of zucchini and tomato before telling her thank you.

Turns out, I liked Casey. We talked about her dogs. She laughed easily in this cute way that wrinkled her nose. As we chatted, the dark vixen fantasy of her that I'd built in my head started to dissolve. Her nails were bitten to the quick and she had crow's feet around her eyes. She made a fart joke, and we both teased Jordan for scrunching his nose.

By the time I needed to leave for class, I found myself wishing I could stay. I left them to polish off the last of the pizza.

Partway to class, I started to feel a rush of optimism, even euphoria. *An open relationship could be fun.* I pulled my scooter over in a parking lot and pulled out my phone to send Jordan a text.

Casey is great. Whatever you want to do on your date, I'm comfortable with it.

As I put my phone in my pocket, I looked up and saw Jordan's car passing by. They must have finished and left right after I did.

Still feeling comfortable? Radio K asked.

Surprisingly, I was.

7

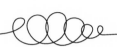

Flirting Is like Skydiving— Quick Thrill, Hard Landing

If Jordan tries to text while he walks, he sometimes stops in his tracks without realizing it. I find it cute, actually—he just gets so caught up in thought that he's all mind and thumbs, and his legs run out of commands.

It happened while we were walking from a downtown bar to a scraggly parking lot, in the dark, at the booty-call hour of ten at night. He got safely across the street and then stalled on the edge of the parking lot. I took a couple paces ahead of him before I realized he'd stopped.

"What's up?" I turned around, watching his brow crease in the small blue light of his screen.

He looked up and gave an exasperated sigh. "I don't know what to write back."

"Let me see."

He handed me his phone. Pulled up on the screen was a text conversation he'd been having with Casey. She'd written something about it being a hot night.

I had an idea, and I stifled a shameless giggle. I pulled up a browser and found an image of a pat of butter melting into a puddle. I pasted it into his text and typed, *I know some things that are hot.*

"Send that," I said, handing his phone back. I watched the smile I'd hoped I'd get spread across his face.

"You're so much better at flirting than me," he said.

It would only occur to me later how weird it must have been to be in Casey's shoes. Did she wonder whether Jordan was sharing her text messages with me? Would she care?

We were so new to the open-relationship thing that these weren't questions I thought to ask. We talked about texts with potential lovers in the same way best friends help each other problem-solve their text threads with their boyfriends and girlfriends—basically, without a second thought to whether someone else's permission or consent might be needed.

When we opened our relationship, we suddenly each became more self-conscious about our phones. For a while, we each kept our message alerts on, until we realized we were interrupting our own dates and movie times with constant dings from back-and-forth texts to other people. Sometimes it was only mildly annoying. Other times it became fuel for jealousy.

Sometimes I'd hear Jordan's phone dinging and reflexively start bashing myself. *Casey is sexier than you, isn't she? She's more confident too. You pretty much suck, you know that?* It didn't take long before we silenced our phones.

Still, texts from other people would light up the screens, distracting our conversations. We started flipping our phones screen-side down.

. . .

After a few weeks of Jordan seeing Casey for casual dates, I started texting Rob.

Rob was flirtatious by nature. I was hanging out with him and a group of friends one night, lounging in a circle of camp chairs around a fire, when he caught my eye and held it just a quarter second longer than usual. A little trill of electricity ran up the side of my neck. I still felt thrilled by his attention even when I realized he gave that kind of flirtatious energy freely to everyone in the circle. He especially did it to Kimberly, who was married to a guy who was away a lot on military duty.

When our circle petered out and everyone crawled into tents, I wormed into a sleeping bag on a tarp on the ground. It wasn't forecasted to rain, and I wanted to watch the stars a bit. Kimberly probably thought I was asleep when she quietly crawled out of her tent and snuck into Rob's.

When we drove back the next day, she sat in the front seat, writing letters to friends and drawing all over them with colored pencils. I looked over her shoulder from time to time. When she got to a letter addressed to her husband, she paused for a long, long time, and eventually made conversation with Rob and put all the letters and pencils away.

One night, when Jordan was out on a date with Casey, I went out dancing with Rob, Kimberly, and a few of our married friends. We went to an outdoor venue where the DJ swung between nineties rap and bachata. I got drunk enough that I started stumbling out of my flip-flops and kicked them off to the side to dance barefoot on the concrete patio, until I got yelled at by a bouncer to put my shoes back on.

Chastised, I slid my feet back into the straps and stomped off to get a gin and tonic. I'd show that bouncer by getting drunker and sloppier—then he'd wish he'd let me just dance it out—and if I cut my feet on a broken beer bottle, so be it.

I took my gin and tonic to a table where Rob was sitting alone, watching Kimberly and the other women dance.

"Not feeling like dancing?" I asked.

He shrugged. "I'm just thinking."

"About Kimberly?"

He looked at me, stunned. I'd surprised myself a little. I hadn't expected to just blurt it out. He raised his eyebrows, opened his mouth to say something, then closed it again. Then he gave me that look, a quarter second too long.

"I need to hang out with women who aren't married," he said.

"Jordan and I just opened our relationship," I said. The words came out before I'd really thought about them. I immediately felt nervous and tossed back the last half of my drink. I willed my face not to pucker at the influx of well gin. "So I guess you never know what's possible until you ask," I said.

Alarm bells went off in my head. *You're telling him too much. He's into Kimberly, not you. You're only embarrassing yourself.* But then, I didn't really care if I was a consolation prize to him. It felt exciting to be bold.

I winked, set my empty glass down, and walked away toward the dancers.

Ugh, a wink, really? Radio K chided. *You have terrible game.*

Most of the friends in our group lost steam somewhere around midnight and went home. The DJ had settled on a long string of overworn early-2000s hits. Rob, Kimberly, and I agreed none of us was ready to sleep. We decided to walk to Rob's house, a few blocks away.

His roommates were awake. We all drank Knob Creek and chit-chatted for a half hour in their living room until Kimberly started yawning. She curled up on one half of the couch. I decided to head out. And Rob, surprisingly, said he wanted to walk me out to my bike.

"You're right; this empty street looks pretty shady," I said when we got to the sidewalk. "Good thing you came out to protect me."

He stood close as I unlocked my bike from the rack, just close enough that I not-so-much-by-accident brushed his shoulder as I stood up and shoved my lock into my bag. We stood there, silence extending for just a quarter second too long.

Until I put my hand behind his neck and pulled his head down to mine. I gave him a quick kiss at first, in case it was an overstep, but he immediately returned the kiss with a much longer one. His hands grazed my hips, and on their way up to my shoulders he brushed the backs of his fingers against my nipple, which imme-diately hardened under my thin cotton dress.

"You should go back inside. Kimberly is waiting for you," I said.

"But you're so much more interesting."

To which my mind replied with two possibilities: *For now*, or *You're lying.*

I didn't care.

I kissed him again, and he held the back of my head. No thoughts, just the feeling of his skin and his lips. It felt blissful to have a blank mind and so many sensations.

Then I came back to myself and remembered Kimberly was inside waiting for him. I put my palm in the middle of his chest and shoved him away.

"Don't be rude. Go back in." I straddled my bike and started to roll down the sidewalk. I looked back over my shoulder. "I'll text you tomorrow; let's meet up."

As I rode away, I was glad he couldn't see my face. I shrieked silently. My heart was pounding. When I turned around the corner, out of sight of his front door, I sat back on the seat and raised my hands in the air to feel the rush of wind around my arms. I suddenly felt like staying up all night, just to get a few more hours of feeling so alive.

I want first kisses over and over again. They always feel so scary and so brave.

. . .

My flirtation with Rob lasted all of two weeks. We went on one date, a hike together to a remote spot, and we sunbathed nude on wide boulders and fooled around a bit. I went down on him, and afterward, he stretched out in the sun and closed his eyes. He didn't reach out to touch me, and I felt embarrassed.

You must have done something wrong just now, Radio K teased. *Either you're really bad at that or he's turned off by your bush. Everyone shaves these days.* I said nothing about wanting to be touched, because I didn't want Rob to confirm that he didn't want to touch me.

We didn't really talk after, except to pick a taco shop to drive to for lunch on our way back into town. We picked at our food while making nervous jokes, and then I dropped him off back at his house. We both said we'd be in touch.

I sexted him a couple of pics in my underwear that he didn't respond to for three days. I kept my cool on day one; I'm a slow texter too. On day two I thought he might be playing coy, and I felt angry and embarrassed. By day three I hoped he'd broken his phone or broken a bone—nothing too serious, just a forearm or something that made it hard to text back. *Why the fuck hasn't someone built in a "delete" feature on text messages?*

Then he texted back saying he'd been on a road trip away from reception. "What a wonderful sight to come back to," he wrote. *Thank god.*

A few days later I invited him out for drinks because I was going to be in his neighborhood for a work function. He said he'd try to make it. I got out of work and wandered around his neighborhood for twenty minutes before he texted to cancel.

In the background of all of that, Jordan and I were gabbing like a couple of giddy schoolgirls. Casey had been texting him erratically and cryptically. Over pizza and pints at a bar, Jordan and I shared our frustrations with flirting and rejection. The bartender kept his eyes averted but he kept polishing the same glass.

It's easy to look back and think, *Wow, you two—take a freaking hint.* It's clear to me now that the people we'd chosen to pursue were uncomfortable. Maybe it was the prospect of dating a partnered person, or maybe they just didn't end up liking each of us as much as they thought they would.

But, like so many people in that exciting, fleeting, early infatuation stage, I only saw those signals through the warped lens of my desperation. *Obviously,* the reason Rob didn't text me back was because he was busy, or he was scared of starting a new relationship too fast, or he thought he needed to play games to entice me. It couldn't be that he just wasn't interested; otherwise, why would he text me back at all, even if it took three or four days?

Each flirtatious text message was another twig to thatch over a hole in my self-worth. A hole into which I'd accidentally dropped my sense of security and my self-confidence.

Much as I was trying to fool myself, I wasn't in it just for the flirtation and the impulsivity. I needed Rob to like me so I could get the high of being someone's new shiny object. I needed the thrill in order to remember I was sexy and desirable.

Things fizzled out with Rob when I tried my next experiment: I decided I wasn't going to text first. It naturally ended without fanfare when it turned out he wasn't going to text first either. Everything just stopped. The next time I went out dancing with my married friends, neither Rob nor Kimberly came.

Jordan's flirtation with Casey fizzled out, too. After a few dates that Jordan described as starting great and ending awkwardly, Casey started ghosting him. She stopped showing up at the bar where she'd been a regular.

And without a word, we all moved on with our lives.

8

The Ex Machina
Drinking Game

"Don't get up so fast."

Stevie and I were at the gym, and I'd tripped and tumbled on top of her. Embarrassed, I moved to lift myself off the mats. She grabbed my hips.

I paused for a second, blood pounding in my ears, wanting to obey her and wanting to get up before anyone saw. I stood up, loudly said something about feeling thankful for the cushion when there are so many clumsy people around, and I held her wrist to help her up.

Later that day, she casually let slip that she and her boyfriend Tyler had an open relationship—a fact I kept repeating to myself on the drive home.

What on earth are you planning to do with that information? Radio K wanted to know. *You barely know what your own vulva looks like— what, you've looked at it in a mirror twice? And you're terrible at fingering yourself. You have no idea what you're doing. Plus, you're not queer.*
At least, I didn't think so.

. . .

Back when I was home for the summer after my first year of college, well before I met Sam, I remember going out to a bar in my hometown to see live music. I must have been eighteen. The lead singer looked like Joan Baez, and she moaned at the mic like she was breaking up with it on every song. She had brown hair that hung in a straight ruler line to her waist, and she would throw her hand through it and cause her hair to flick in furious waves.

And I shit you not, her name was *Tiger.*

The whole set, I stared at Tiger. And when her bass player wasn't hanging his head in that moody way rock bassists do, he was staring at me. The set ended with a frenzied rendition of "The Chain" by Fleetwood Mac, and Tiger sounded just like Stevie Nicks, her voice raspy and powerful.

I really want to flirt with her. The thought snuck into my brain without asking and refused to budge. *Is it just that I admire her?* No, I knew it wasn't that. I get nervous around people I admire, but this was something else. I didn't want to *be* her; I *wanted* her. I could tell by the way my eyes traveled across her waist.

I walked up to her, chirped something like "That was so good!" and then, when the bass player caught my eye again, I beelined to him.

He was cute and tall. He sipped a Modelo Negra, so he had to be a couple of years older than me. I told him I loved "The Chain." He said he hated that song and hated Fleetwood Mac.

Must have been Tiger's pick, I thought. I listened to *Rumours* on repeat for the rest of the summer. The bass player became my boyfriend for that summer, and every time he heard *Rumours* in my car, he rolled his eyes.

Despite how flustered I'd gotten around Tiger, I didn't recognize then what I see so clearly now: *you're queer, honey.* Instead, I promptly got a boyfriend to erase the thought.

I'd had the same sensation just a few months earlier, at move-in day at my dorm. I collected the key to my new apartment in a college-owned building in downtown Chicago, then I filed into an elevator with my parents, and there she was.

Janie had black hair with short bangs, and she wore a black-and-white-striped boatneck top that made her look very Parisian, and on top of it all she had beautiful lips like a perfect sliced plum and big doe eyes with dense lashes. Both our sets of parents were crowded in the elevator with us. In my imagination, I pressed Janie into a corner of the elevator to make out with her, with her hands pinned behind her waist.

In reality, I caught her eye for about a quarter of a second and then looked down to where a black smudge of gum was polished into the dingy cracks of the elevator floor.

The elevator dinged at my floor. My parents and I stepped out. Janie and her parents stepped out on my floor. We all walked down to the same apartment number.

I almost died.

Janie was going to be my roommate. Later that day, we met our other roommate, Margo, who had heavy-lidded feline eyes that she accentuated with eyeliner. Within the week, we were thick as thieves.

They smoked, so I'd always buy them a pack of cigarettes, smoke half of one, and feel sick. I also brought them hash browns and green juice in the morning to nurse their hangovers. They were punk rockers, I was a nurturer, and maybe I brought them stuff to ingratiate myself to them so they'd keep showing me the glorious wonders of being a bad girl.

They both had crushes on our neighbor, Kyle. Margo later dated him; Janie didn't. We had many whiskey-and-nicotine-fueled nights about it all.

In Kyle's apartment were the first times I ever stayed up an entire night, got drunk, smoked pot, and got rejected in the middle of sex, by one of his roommates. I'd nursed a crush on the roommate all semester, and on the night he finally moved to go down on me, I was so excited that I lay there completely still and silent, my body thrumming with nerves, too afraid to make a sound that would break the spell. After a minute, he sat back up, said, "you're too green," pulled on his clothes, and left. To this day I have no idea what the fuck it means to be green.

When Margo's nineteenth birthday came up, we decided to road-trip to Canada to drink legally. Our friend Shaw had a tiny, shitty car whose steering wheel shook while going down the highway at any speeds between fifty-five and eighty-two. When I got pulled over for going eighty-five, the policewoman was incredibly nonplussed at my explanation that I *had* to go that fast or the car would vibrate my hands off.

I remember nothing of visiting Toronto at nineteen except that we were too broke to go anywhere that wasn't a dive. We wanted to find some packed nightclub with strobes and multicolored lights lasering through the air. Instead, we found a basement spot with a knot of about fifteen people dancing in a dark corner.

Janie and Margo did shots and ran into the middle of the pack to dance with their arms waving in the air. Shaw ordered a pint and sat with one elbow propped on the bar, looking out at the cluster.

I ordered a Corona with lime, because it was the only beer I'd ever seen my mom drink, and she always put a sliver of lime in it. I squeezed the lime into the pony neck of my bottle, poking it with my finger to pop it down until the head volcanoed up over the rim. I wasn't expecting that and quickly slurped up the foam, hoping no one noticed I didn't know what I was doing.

The song "Maps" by the Yeah Yeah Yeahs came on. I fucking love this song. And there was Janie, wearing a torn Slayer T-shirt, half-grown-out hand-chopped bangs hanging over her eyes, pumping her knee to the beat while Karen O sang in her husky broken grace, and goddamn, I wanted to kiss Janie. She looked up as I approached and dramatically pantomimed the words. "Wait…they don't love you like I love you," she whisper-sang as she reached out for me. I knew it was a joke. I wanted it to be true.

If there was any single moment at which I could have recognized that I might be in love with women, it would have been that one. I remember secretly wishing that when I joined the circle, she would wrap her arms around my neck and plant her plum lips on mine. Instead, she turned to Kyle, who was dancing with Margo.

By the time we got back from Toronto, Margo was dating Kyle, Janie was hung up on Kyle, and I'd convinced myself my attraction to Janie was a strange drunken urge that had already passed.

You're not queer, Radio K teased. *You're just lonely.*

. . .

The Ex Machina Drinking Game finally gave me the courage to kiss Stevie. She and Tyler invited Jordan and me to a movie night, and as we parked on the street, Stevie came running out with a bottle of Maker's Mark that she rapped on my passenger window.

Given the nature of the Ex Machina Drinking Game, you may not be surprised to know that I cannot recall the plot of the movie *Ex Machina* with any reliable accuracy. In any case, the plot doesn't matter. The main character is named Caleb. Even though there are only four characters in the movie, anytime one of them addresses Caleb, they say his name.

In the Ex Machina Drinking Game, you take a swig of whiskey every time someone says Caleb's name, which occurs at a rate of approximately two repetitions per minute. I can attest to this calculation, because within the first five minutes or so, my lips went numb. Halfway into the movie, I was hammered.

As I got drunker, I let my limbs get a little sloppier on purpose: when I handed the bottle to Stevie, I let my hand drop and rest on her hip.

I did not care who Caleb was or what was about to happen to him.

We were watching the movie in Tyler's bedroom, where there was a huge TV. Tyler and Stevie had invited Jordan and me over for the movie, but there was no other furniture in the bedroom, so we all lay on the bed. My arm pressed against Stevie's arm.

I couldn't look at her. The whiskey had loosened up my body and made me physically careless, but my mind was still whirring about a thousand miles per hour. *Could I kiss her, or no? Should I ask first? Does my mouth move funny when I make out with people? Will it move funny now since I can't feel my lips? How long is the right amount of time to look her in the eye? What if I look too long and make her feel awkward? What if I do anything that makes her feel awkward? How the hell does anyone, anywhere, ever pluck up the courage to make out with someone?*

We watched the entire movie lying with our arms at our sides, like when I'm in a middle seat on an airplane and feeling too polite to use the armrests for fear of brushing up against a stranger. We speculated for a drunken minute or two about the weird note the movie leaves off on. *Was Ava just manipulating everyone the entire time?* And then, maybe because Tyler recognized the awkward haze of inhibition still lingering in the room, he put on reruns of *Rick and Morty*.

Jordan, Stevie, and Tyler thought *Rick and Morty* was hilarious. I hate this show. I have a hard time with cartoons in general; all the voices are just too loud and grating, and almost all the humor is built on sarcasm.

I do not speak sarcasm as a native tongue. It takes me several seconds to translate it—I have to sort out whether a sarcastic comment is meant as an attack or a joke, and it's usually a mix of both, and then I have to decode the different elements of it to figure out how nasty the attack is and whether I can let myself think it's funny. Then there's another whole process of analyzing the literary merits of the sarcasm to understand whether it warrants a laugh. It's a whole rigamarole.

The deeper truth is, I hate sarcasm because the people who use it are always trying to prove that the thing they're making fun of is worthless. Because I often believed I was worthless, I took sarcasm literally to prove my own belief to myself. Then I took my anger out on the speaker, and everyone would tell me to take it easy; after all, it was just a joke. It never felt like a joke.

Jordan is sarcastic. He helps me with this. Even so, he can't magically make *Rick and Morty* funny to me. Everyone yells hurtful things all the time.

Jordan, Stevie, and Tyler were busting up laughing. I was bored and annoyed. And maybe that was the final motivator for me to lean over and plant a long kiss on Stevie's tulip of a mouth.

She kissed me enthusiastically back, like she'd been waiting for me to be brave. Her hand slid under my shirt. She turned to Tyler and made out with him, her hand on the button of my jeans. Jordan stroked my back. The four of us started to move wordlessly through a choreography, with Stevie and I kissing our boyfriends and then turning back to each other.

The inane voices of *Rick and Morty* were still yelling at each other in the background, but my head was buzzing with white noise. Every place Stevie's fingers touched me lit up like a Lite-Brite. I wanted her soft petite mouth on everything. I wanted mine on everything.

I thought, naively, that I would magically be great at lady sex, but I'd never seen another vulva besides mine, and Stevie was shaped differently. Her clit was so tiny I wasn't quite sure I was on the right spot. I couldn't tell if she liked the same kinds of touch I did. She was silent when I stroked one way, and silent when I stroked the other direction. Silent when I picked up speed and silent when I slowed down.

She pulled at my arms to bring my face up, level with hers, and smiled as she licked her fingers and felt around my clit. I made so much noise Jordan put his hand over my mouth so I wouldn't wake the neighbor on the other side of the duplex wall.

No one spoke. We all got by with nonverbal communication: goosebumps, a lift in the hips, a craning of the neck, fingers that pulled in for more, more, more.

By the time things started to wind down, I still couldn't tell if Stevie had come. Coward that I was, I didn't ask her.

But I did ask Jordan, later when we were alone, whether he also thought it was difficult to find her clit. He said he did not have an issue.

I was ashamed I couldn't pluck up the courage to ask Stevie what she liked or what she wanted. But I was even more terrified that I'd finally made a move on a woman I liked, and she wouldn't like me back. Now that I'd acted on my desire, I worried something fundamental would change—in my friendship with Stevie and in my understanding of myself.

I woke up with a cracking hangover. All day my head pounded with a splitting headache and my heart raced. *Where the hell do I go from here?*

9

The Worst Lie
I Ever Told (Part 1)

Even though Jordan was the first one to say he wanted to date other people, I was the first one to go off on my own and have sex with someone else.

It wasn't with Stevie. I didn't have the guts to see if I could impress her on my own.

Instead, I asked Tyler if he wanted to hang out for an afternoon. Stevie was cool with it.

I wasn't sure if I was going to sleep with him on my own, so I didn't tell Jordan I was definitely going to. I asked Jordan whether he'd be comfortable with us "fooling around." Jordan said yes.

And this is how I learned that vague phrasing is like a fender-bender: the crunch in the bumper doesn't seem like a big deal until you take it to the mechanic and he tells you the car is totaled because the whole frame is misaligned.

So Tyler and I met up for lunch, and over lunch we each had a cocktail. After lunch we decided to walk back to his house, where I'd parked my scooter. It was a half mile away. It happened to be a half mile packed with bars. We thought it would be a fun idea to hit up the favorites on the walk back, a Saturday afternoon cocktail crawl.

Looking back, I cringe at how this seemed like a fun idea. But I wanted to sleep with Tyler, and I was afraid of my desire at the same time. So I agreed to more drinks, hoping they would quiet the part of myself that felt anxious to take a step I couldn't take back. In half a mile, I got stumble-drunk blitzed. By then, the idea of sleeping with each other sounded reckless and exciting.

When I'd flirted with Rob, he was excited for my attention but didn't seem all that excited about me. As I tripped up the steps of Tyler's place, he seemed to *want me*.

The room was spinning pleasantly. A kind of terror crept into the edges of my attention—*what the fuck are you doing, is there any coming back from this point, please please don't jump, just walk around the block fifty times to sober up or call a cab to drive you home*—but I shoved it down somewhere. I'm a pro at compartmentalizing.

There was a more immediate whisper filling my ears, a silky serpent-and-the-apple kind of voice saying, *There are no real rules in life. You can do anything. Just see what happens.*

It was a hot summer day, and I made some joke about how Tyler could fry an egg on my stomach, like Charlie Sheen in *Hot Shots*. Then I talked about how Spike Lee's character rubbed Rosie

Perez's character down with an ice cube in *Do the Right Thing*. I was nervous and chatting too fast.

Tyler went to the freezer and came back with an ice cube in his mouth. He rolled the ice cube across my arms, then my chest, then my stomach. The ice cube was cold, and his lips were warm, and the contrast sent goosebumps across my skin.

Tyler and I hadn't touched each other the previous night when we'd all fooled around; Stevie and I had mostly focused on each other. The sex with Tyler wasn't amazing, but it was *new*, and my skin and my brain lit up with the excitement of learning a new body and touch from different hands.

The swooping feeling in my head started to settle into a dull headache. I closed my eyes and focused on the sensations on my skin.

When the sex was over, I felt very sober. Tyler put on music, and he seemed to want to hang out. I got dressed quickly. The techno beats sounded too dark and weird. I wanted to be alone. I got on my scooter and took the long way home. I wanted to buy myself time to think.

What will change now? Was that worth it?

My brain was totally blank. I couldn't come up with an answer.

* * *

Jordan was home when I got back. He seemed freaked out. His eyes were wide, his gestures just a little bit twitchy. He kept maybe half an inch more distance than he usually did. He asked how the date was, and I said it was good. He asked if we had sex.

I said no.

Jordan got in the shower, and I followed him into the bathroom. Panic flooded across my skin like a scalding pot of water being poured over the crown of my head.

Why the fuck did I say no?

I was being a coward and saving my goddamned hide; that's why.

Jordan had looked so upset when I walked in, and I assumed I knew the video that had been playing in his head all day. I realized immediately that asking for permission to "fool around" was not at all the same as asking directly and clearly if he was okay with me having sex with someone else. And when I said no, I hadn't slept with Tyler, the lie had exactly the effect I'd wanted: his face softened, his shoulders relaxed a little, and it seemed like things would be okay.

About twenty seconds into his shower, I peeled the curtain back. "I did have sex with Tyler. I was afraid to tell the truth earlier," I said.

His face—it's heartbreak all over again remembering his face in the next moment. It twisted back and forth between pain and sorrow, not fully landing on either but on some confused combination in between.

"Why did you lie?" he asked.

"I was scared. I took the coward's way out for a minute."

Jordan looked away. He turned off the water in the shower, whipped the curtain back, and pulled a towel off the rack. He smashed the towel against his face for several moments. His shoulders shook a little.

"It was just a minute," I said quickly. "I didn't want to hide it from you. I'm sorry."

He lowered the towel but didn't dry himself off. He just stood there, frozen.

"Why didn't you give me time to adjust? Take baby steps? Why did you jump all the way into having sex with him?"

"I don't know," I said, which was a lie. I did know. My reasons just didn't seem like enough.

We'd spent months taking baby steps. We'd gone on several dates with other people. We'd already slept with Stevie and Tyler together. Jordan had nearly had sex with Casey on one date and got cold feet at the last moment. I thought we were ready for bigger steps, but now that it seemed like Jordan's trust in me was crashing down, the idea that we were ready seemed stupid. Heartless.

Jordan stood there, naked. I wanted to dry him off. To put him in warm clothes and put him to bed and for us to wake up in the morning with the memory of this day erased.

"Didn't you think of me?" he asked.

"I thought about how excited I was that we're taking this leap to experiment together. That we're defining for ourselves what our relationship looks like," I said.

Part of me legitimately felt that way. I'd liked the feeling of being on a first date again. Of not knowing what turns the other person on or off, of playing around until I found the switch.

But the explanation seemed flimsy now that Jordan was hurt. My heart broke. I'd been thinking of me, not him. *I hate myself.*

I suddenly wanted the conversation to end as quickly as possible.

"I'm so sorry," I said.

"I feel sick." Jordan wrapped the towel around his waist and leaned against the counter. He hung his head and didn't look at me. I stared at the top of his head in the mirror.

"I'm really sorry," I said again.

"Did you use protection?"

"Yes."

Jordan shook his head, then looked up. "That night I almost had sex with Casey, I couldn't do it because I couldn't stop thinking about you."

Jordan couldn't have sex with someone else without you, and somehow you could, Radio K whispered. *What does that say about you?* I gave in and answered the way he expected. *It says I don't care about him the way he deserves.*

A smaller, quieter part of me knew that wasn't true. She knew I loved Jordan and that I was capable of loving him and being reckless at the same time. She tried to tell me as much in that moment, but I refused to listen to her. I was too busy hating myself the way I thought I deserved.

"I'm sorry," I said again. I hated that I could think of nothing else to say.

"I have to get ready," Jordan said. He finally looked up and robotically hung the towel back on the rack, walking to the bedroom to get clothes.

"Oh shit, I forgot," I said. We were planning to go to a party that night with Stevie and Tyler. Worse, it was an underwear party at a bar with an outdoor courtyard. The idea had seemed fun at the time: celebrate a hot summer night with an optional clothing check and the opportunity to see hot bodies stripped down in their bare essentials. There was going to be a sandbox and a waterslide. Before that afternoon, I'd thought the party would be sexy and fun. Now I was horrified at the idea.

"We can cancel," I said.

"No, let's go." Jordan put on a pair of tie-dyed underwear that made his ass look particularly cute. He pulled on jeans and opened a drawer full of T-shirts and stared at it. He didn't look at me, even though I hovered a few feet away. "It doesn't matter what I pick; I'm just going to take it off right away anyway," he grumbled, and grabbed the first shirt on top. "Please stop staring at me," he added.

"Sorry," I said one last time.

＊ ＊ ＊

When we got to the party, Stevie wasn't there. Tyler said she'd join us when she got off work in an hour. Jordan and Tyler greeted each other like nothing had happened, and I felt a glimmer of hope. *Maybe things can settle and feel normal again with a little time.*

Keep dreaming, princess, Radio K shot back. *Everyone is just pretending.*

I slid my dress over my head to hand to the clothing check person and took my ticket. I deliberately looked away from Tyler. I didn't want to know if he was looking at me. I held Jordan's hand and looked at his face to see if I could read whether he was doing okay. He didn't look back. I scanned the crowd for anyone else I might know, anyone who could help us all talk about something other than the day that kept running over and over through my mind.

Jordan spotted a coworker of his, and we all quickly dived into a conversation about climbing. I chugged my beer as quickly as I could and got us all another round.

It seemed like everyone in the crowd was drunker than on a usual Saturday night. Maybe it was that everyone needed extra liquid courage to feel comfortable in their underwear. By the time Stevie showed up, I'd managed to feel a few short stretches of stumbly happiness. Jordan had smiled at me at least twice. We danced chest to chest and Jordan shimmied in a deliberately awkward way that made me laugh. Things were going to be okay.

Stevie had the sexiest underwear, with several delicate black straps tracing lines around her chest and hips, and she wanted to dance with me. For the rest of the night, Jordan and his coworker and Tyler and Stevie and I danced together in a chain, holding each other's hips.

I made out with Jordan on the dance floor and strangers called us sexy. *We are adaptable after all*, I thought. *Maybe my mistakes were just mistakes and not catastrophes.*

The bartenders called out last call over the PA system, but everyone kept dancing. They had to turn on floodlights to break the spell.

10

Here Are All the Things
I Wasn't Going to Tell You

Stevie had to work the next day. But we all remembered that a mutual friend of ours who had a pool was out of town and had told us to use it whenever. Jordan, Tyler, and I decided to go swimming. We thought it would help smooth things over to hang out together.

Jordan set a six-pack on the patio table. Tyler had a fifth of Jameson. We all smoked weed. The pool water got all sparkly, and everything seemed funny to me. I laughed easily. A friend from the neighborhood showed up, got high, and immediately commandeered a circular pool float to lounge in. We each cracked a beer, stripped down, and got in the pool.

Jordan sat on the steps, chest deep, elbows resting on the lip of the pool. I was enjoying the heightened sensation of water swirling across my skin, so I swam a couple of laps, diving down to the bottom of the pool to feel the change in pressure.

I surfaced next to a pool float. It was a floating lounge chair, and Tyler was already holding on to it, his arms folded and his head resting on his forearms. I decided to steal it from him. In a big splash, I leapt up and sat on the chair. Tyler smirked and went underwater.

A moment later, his head was under my back, pushing up on the chair to flip it. I fell into the water but held on to the sides of the chair. Tyler jumped on top of it, his chest lying across it, and I tried to twist the chair to flip him over, but I couldn't get enough leverage. I let go.

Across the pool, Jordan was no longer leaning back against the edge of the pool. His arms were by his sides in the water, and he was sitting with his knees tucked up by his chest. I swam over and sat on the steps next to him.

"There's another pool float," he said, and pointed to a little inflated donut that was floating next to the passed-out neighbor.

"I know," I shrugged. "It's fun to fight for the better one."

Jordan was silent for a few minutes. Then he got out of the pool. "I'm going to get another beer. Want one?"

I shook my head. I was still feeling plenty high, and I had a hunch that a beer would start to make me feel nauseous and sad. Tyler paddled over to the edge of the pool, got out, and poured Jameson and Coke into a plastic cup. I swam fast over to the abandoned float, rolled up onto it, and paddled to Jordan, who was back at the steps.

"Got it," I said. He gave a half-hearted nod.

Tyler jumped into the pool just close enough to push one side of the float down and tip me out. He scrambled up onto it. I didn't fight him this time. I was by the side of the pool, so I held on to the edge and pushed the float away with my foot. Then I sat back down by Jordan.

"Are you having a good time?" I asked.

He grunted in a way that sounded vaguely positive, but he said nothing.

A few minutes later, Tyler slid off the pool float and stood with his arms along the side of the pool. He started telling a story about wrestling with a guy at his gym, and how he'd beaten the guy by the skin of his teeth.

"He put me in a headlock, and he thought he had me, but I got out of it. Kicked out his legs and got him on the mat," Tyler was saying. He was talking so fast, but not fully enunciating his words. In rapid fire, he described how he pinned the guy, but I couldn't follow.

"How do you get out of a headlock?" I asked.

"You tuck your chin so they can't get their arm under your jaw, and then you slide your hands like this—" he tried to demonstrate in the air, but then he stopped himself. "Here, let me show you."

I went over and wrapped my arm around his neck, and he slipped out of my arm in just a few seconds. I still didn't get it.

"Let's switch," he said, and before I could ask another question, Tyler had his arm wrapped around my neck. Then he dunked me under the water.

I immediately freaked out. His arm was tight around my throat. I tried to slide my fingers under his elbow, but he was holding on too tight. I pulled at his arm. He didn't budge. Panicked, I clawed under his arm with my fingernails. I tapped him on the chest, the signal for *Stop now, I'm out.*

Still, he didn't budge.

I knew I could hold my breath longer if I could get myself to calm down, but I couldn't calm down. *Why the fuck isn't he responding?*

I shoved my elbow as hard as I could into his ribs. Finally, a few seconds later, he released his arm. I shot up from the water and stood there shaking and gasping.

Jordan was close by now. His eyes were wide. "Are you okay?" he asked.

"Yeah, I'm fine," I lied. "I just couldn't figure it out. How do you get your fingers under someone's arm? You were holding me too tight."

"Try again," Tyler said, and he reached for me. I heard Jordan say, "No, don't!" But then Tyler's arm was around my neck, and he pulled me under again.

I tried to wiggle my fingers under his arm to push his elbow up from under my face, but he was holding me even tighter this time, so tightly I wondered if I might accidentally pass out. I clawed at his arm, shoved him in the ribs, reached up above the water and slapped him in the chest, twisted my body so I could try to push his chest away. He just held me there.

I started to get really, really scared. I couldn't get him to budge. My mind flashed back to his face as he grabbed me. His eyes had looked unfocused. I was pretty sure the reason he wasn't responding to me was because he was incredibly drunk. I dug my nails into his arm. The muscles around my ribs spasmed.

Tyler finally let go again, and I resurfaced, coughing. Jordan was standing there with his arms outstretched like he was about to grab Tyler. The neighbor was still floating at the other end of the pool, a hat over his eyes. I got out of the pool and got dressed before I was fully dried off.

"Do you want to go?" Jordan said, his eyes still wide.

Tyler was so drunk his eyelids were getting heavy as he stood there in the pool. I looked over at the neighbor again. He seemed totally unconcerned. *Was this not a big deal?* My hands were still a little shaky. I didn't feel normal. No one in this pool looked normal. I didn't know what to do.

"No, you guys swim as long as you want. I'm feeling waterlogged."

"I think I'm done too," Jordan said.

Tyler was staring off into space. Jordan got out and started toweling himself down. Then Tyler announced he had to pee, and he walked slowly up the pool steps and over to a tucked-away corner of the yard where we couldn't see him.

I sat down at the patio table, and my eyes landed on the bottle of Jameson. It had been full when we got here, and now it was nearly gone. Tyler had been the only one drinking it. Jordan got dressed and sat down at the patio table, and we waited. Several minutes ticked by and Tyler didn't come back.

I walked around the pool to the other side of the yard, and there was Tyler, still standing at the spot where he'd peed. He was swaying on his heels.

"Come on, let's go," I said, but he didn't turn around or acknowledge he'd heard me. I grabbed him by the shoulders. "Come *on*," I said again, and he stumbled against me. I walked him back to the patio table. I wanted to shove him into the pool and leave him there.

Instead, Jordan and I helped him get dressed. The neighbor finally got out of the pool, grabbed the few beers he had left, and waved goodbye. Jordan and I walked Tyler to Jordan's car and drove him home, where I unlocked Tyler's door for him and helped him to bed. I left the key on his desk and closed the door. I wanted to kick it in, and at the same time I was so tired.

"He's so drunk," I said when I got back in the car. I tried to make my tone sound casual.

"He drank almost that whole bottle by himself," Jordan said. His voice was flat. He looked straight ahead out the windshield.

"Are you okay?" I asked.

Jordan shook his head a little. "I was starting to feel okay about you sleeping with him. Last night I thought it really would feel okay and I just needed time. But today was really upsetting. I don't trust him."

I don't trust him either, I thought, but I didn't say anything. I questioned my judgment in picking Tyler, but I didn't want to hear Jordan question my judgment, and I had a feeling that was coming. So I stared straight ahead and said nothing.

"Are you okay?" Jordan asked.

"I'm fine," I said, but my voice rose on the last word and give me away.

●　●　●

The next day I called Tyler and told him I was really upset about what happened at the pool.

He didn't remember anything at all. He'd blacked out, he said. *No shit.* Tyler listened quietly while I described that he'd held me in a chokehold underwater and that I'd felt unsafe. I didn't give details.

I did not say I thought I could have drowned. In fact, I rationalized that possibility in my head. *Everyone knows CPR; they would have been able to bring me back if I'd passed out. I would have been fine; what's the big deal?*

"I'm sorry, Em," Tyler said into the phone.

And then silence. I tried to read into that silence the emotions I wanted to hear. I wanted to hear his shame, his guilt, his grief. I felt ashamed. I couldn't tell if he did, but I wanted him to.

Tyler didn't sound horrified to hear about it. And because he remembered nothing, his apology felt meaningless to me.

When I later described what happened to Stevie, she said, "You should have just punched him in the face." All I could think—but didn't say—was, *How in the fuck is that my responsibility?* But the reality was it hadn't crossed my mind to defend myself that forcefully. I didn't feel that powerful.

Was I supposed to shrug it off as dumb drunken horseplay? *How is no one else freaking out about this?*

I know why: because I was the one describing it. I was controlling the story. And I was couching it in all kinds of soft terms to keep from accusing, blaming, and showing my anger.

I was the one who'd put myself in that situation. *I* was the one who didn't stand up for myself. *I* was the one who'd chosen this guy in the first place, *I* was the one with a shitty judge of character, and maybe that was because I didn't have any integrity either.

I felt so embarrassed and helpless that I took all the blame for that onto myself and presented a really controlled, mild front to everyone else. They didn't know how serious it was to me because I didn't tell them.

Instead, I privately promised myself I would never again be around Tyler while he was drunk.

I did, however, agree to go climbing with him the next day. Jordan had to work, but I had the day off. Jordan looked dumbstruck when I told him.

"Why..." Jordan started, and then redirected his question. "Is that what you want to do?" He didn't look at my face. I didn't look him in the eye either. I stared at the back wall of our yard and the bougainvillea I'd planted there two weeks ago. It was dying, shedding all its hot pink flowers onto the dirt.

I'd been climbing with Tyler many times before, and he was always kind and supportive. There were times I'd stood at the bottom of a route, wanting to tackle it and feeling afraid, and Tyler had patiently walked me through, step by step. He told me he'd catch me, and he always had.

I couldn't fit my experiences with him together. He'd protected me, and then he put me in danger. *Could I have known somehow that he would turn on me?* I felt naive and stupid.

And I felt angry. Somehow, I thought that meeting Tyler face-to-face again would help me understand how he could be so careful yet so reckless. How *I* could be so careful and reckless. I wanted to prove to myself that I was strong. That I was unaffected. It was a total lie, but it's what I wanted at that moment.

"He's a good belayer," I said, and swallowed the lump in my throat. "I just need to see him in person so I can feel more resolved about this."

Under the surface, I was freaked out and feeling vulnerable. I wanted Tyler to somehow turn back time, erase the last day, and protect me again.

"I don't think you should go," Jordan said.

I bristled. "I don't think it's okay for either of us to dictate who we hang out with. I'm not going to sleep with him again. I have no desire for that. And I never again want to be around him when he's drinking. I just need to get a sense of him as a friend again."

Jordan took a breath, and then he nodded. I could tell he didn't really agree. But the next day, he went to work, and I went to climb with Tyler.

"Please text me when you're heading back, okay?" Jordan said. He looked worried, his eyes darting around a little as he looked at me. I agreed.

Tyler acted like nothing had happened. In a quiet voice, I told him how freaked out I'd been. He apologized again. I still didn't feel okay about it, but I could tell it was a black hole in his memory, and when I didn't hear the sense of shame I wanted to hear in his voice, I felt helpless all over again. I stopped bringing it up. We focused on climbing. I picked a route that was way too hard for me and threw myself into it until I was panting from the effort. My forearms were so sore I couldn't squeeze my fingers into a fist anymore.

When we both got home, Jordan asked me how it went, his eyes wide.

"It was fine," I said.

"Did he say anything more about the other day?"

"No," I shrugged. "He doesn't remember anything. It just felt like a normal climbing day. It felt good to feel normal."

Jordan pressed his lips together and nodded softly. "I could see that."

. . .

I could count on my hands the number of times Jordan and I had sex in the year that followed. I had constant heartburn and headaches. Sometimes Jordan made advances and I made excuses, complaining that I didn't feel well. I suddenly felt acutely how much physical intimacy is a loss of control, and I wanted to be in total control of my body. I wanted to desire nothing.

Sometimes I spooned Jordan and put a hand over his chest, hoping to feel him relax a little. He would sigh, but his breath would come out all at once like his ribs were too heavy. *You're stressing him out,* I told myself again and again, and retreated to my side of the bed.

Neither of us went to therapy. I knew we needed to talk more—about me having sex with Tyler, about the day at the pool, about how Jordan and I weren't having sex—but I quickly felt overwhelmed anytime Jordan initiated conversations about it. I shut down and told him I needed time to think.

But I never actually took the time to think about it, because I didn't want to feel the panic and helplessness that rose up every time I remembered that day.

I can see now that I craved new partners and thrilling experiences because they cut through the anxious self-censoring jabber in my head. When I got attention from someone new, I felt seen for a moment. When they wanted to kiss me or touch me, I felt desired, validated, *worthy.*

The moment in the pool had flipped that feeling on its head. *You are so worthless,* Radio K snarled. *Look how easily you become a prop in a drunkard's game.*

I didn't accept the parts of myself that had wanted to sleep with Tyler, the parts of myself that were drawn to someone who could dissociate so thoroughly. I wasn't in touch with my own dissociation. And I never brought the conversation back up.

. . .

Months later, when we went to visit my family for Christmas, I felt the most alone I've maybe ever felt. I was surrounded by all the people I love the most, and all I could think about was everything I was unwilling to tell them: how much pain I'd caused, how little I'd thought through that date with Tyler, how much it was shaping the hollow, numb months that had followed. I stopped being myself in front of the people I love, which means I stopped being myself, period.

I'm really close with my mom, but I couldn't tell her all *that*—the flirting with other people, the sex, the pool. I especially didn't know how to explain—to her or to anyone else—how I'd created such pain on a stupid whim to feel the thrill of being chosen by someone else.

Opening our relationship had seemed fun, adventurous, and sexy at first, but now it seemed reckless and repulsive. I was disgusted with myself, and I couldn't bear to see my parents or my brother mirror my disgust back to me.

When my mom asked how I was doing, I said "fine" in a chipper voice and told her I wanted to make yet another batch of Christmas cookies. At least if we were in the kitchen listening to music, I could feel some sense of home and warmth. With my hands busy, I didn't feel like I had to find something to talk about.

Jordan spent most of his downtime on the living room couch, looking at his phone. I felt weird that he was always in the other room. I hoped no one would ask me if everything was okay, because I didn't know how to answer.

We stayed up late with my brother one night, watching some zombie apocalypse comedy. I barely registered the plot because I was looking out of the corner of my eye the entire time, registering any little laugh or breath from Jordan that might indicate he was enjoying himself. His face was totally neutral and unreadable in the dim light from the screen.

The only scene I remember is one in which a bunch of beachgoers ran into the ocean to get away from the zombies and a woman in a string bikini got snatched up by a zombie that tore her head off. My brother cackled. Jordan clenched his jaw and exhaled heavily through his nose.

I stiffened and didn't move my head, even though I wanted to look away. I knew the scene was supposed to be funny, but it felt too real: girl runs into water and loses her head.

11

The One-Dick Policy

"Elsie is cute," Jordan said, and I nodded. I hadn't caught my breath enough to talk yet. We were backpacking up a steep hillside, and my pack was digging into my shoulders. It was the tail end of winter, still cold enough to pull the extra heat off my skin. We stopped at the crest of a hill, and I took a deep breath. I felt good for the first time in months.

Elsie was ahead of us. I liked her a lot. She was funny in a gentle way; she never mocked others to make people laugh. She was a homesteader, and her kitchen counter was always crowded with jars of sourdough starter and fermenting kombucha and mead. She made her own cheese and pickles. And she had a perfect ass.

We stopped at the crest of a hill. "Are you interested in her?" Jordan asked.

I took a moment to think while I wrestled a water bottle out of my pack. For the past few months, Elsie's boyfriend had been away for work. I thought Elsie had mentioned they'd given each other hall passes while they were apart.

I took a sip of water. "Is that on the table?"

Jordan nodded. "I'm feeling okay to explore other relationships again."

"Wow, okay," I said, and smiled. It was the first time outside relationships had come up in months. I felt a little excited. *So things are better with us.*

I looked out to where Elsie was hiking ahead with another friend. They were far enough away that they'd become ants on the hillside. "Do you just mean seeing someone together, or are you feeling okay with us dating people individually too?"

"Both, I guess," Jordan said.

"It's just—we haven't talked about dating other people again since…" I trailed off, not willing to bring the Pool Incident back to mind. "You're okay with me seeing other people on my own?"

"I think I'd be okay with you seeing women."

"But not men," I said flatly.

Jordan looked me in the eye, then looked away.

"It's not that I'm interested in other men," I said. "I'm not even attracted to other men right now."

This was true. I used to like making eye contact with men across crowded bars and airports and sidewalks, but in the last several months, anytime I walked in a room, my eyes gravitated toward women. I found myself edging away from men in crowded places. "But isn't it the same risk to a relationship, dating a man versus a woman?"

"I can't explain it. I don't know why. I just don't feel jealous at the idea of you having a relationship with another woman."

"It just seems sexist," I said. It was easier to talk about sexism than to try to talk about Tyler.

"Maybe it is. I'm sorry," Jordan added. "Over time, I might feel differently. It's just the way I feel right now. I know it's not fair."

I shrugged. I had no desire to date other men anyway; did the principle of it really matter? For the moment, things felt okay. "Feelings aren't fair or unfair. They just are. I think any arrangement is fair if it's what we both choose."

I stopped for a moment and looked down at the pine needles on the trail, thinking. "As a long-term rule, it would feel weird to say we can date other people, but I can only date women. I'd want to work on what that means to both of us. But for right now, that feels fine. I'm excited at the idea of dating women." I looked across the ridge to where Elsie and the other friend were making their way to the base of the cliff. "With Elsie, do you mean date her together?"

Jordan nodded. I shoved my water bottle back in my pack and we started walking again.

"If her relationship with Andy is open, I'd totally go for her."

"I would too," Jordan said. "You should ask her."

"Why me?" Truth was, I was still nervous to pursue anyone. I didn't want to be the one to fuck everything up again.

"Because when a guy from a couple asks another woman out, it can seem creepy. I think it's easier to talk about if it comes from you."

"Okay." I squirmed and adjusted the shoulder straps of my pack.

That day as we set up camp, I found little moments to ask Elsie about her relationship, whether it was open (it was), and how she and her partner had navigated that (well, it seemed). I chickened out of asking her on a three-way date.

Later that week, Elsie approached Jordan and invited us both to dinner at her house. I agonized over what to wear. We'd been friends with Elsie for a while, and she'd seen me grungy and sweaty with stringy hair, sleepless from a night in the woods. I told myself I didn't need to impress her, but I carefully picked out a clingy skirt that wasn't too dressy. I wanted to look comfortable and unfazed about how I looked, even though I was neither of those things.

Over dinner, we talked openly about sleeping together, when we'd last been tested, what the ground rules were in our relationships, what we wanted. Then Elsie led us into her bedroom, she and I sat on her bed, and she kissed me. Jordan bent down and kissed her. She pulled her own dress over her head.

The three of us had the kind of beautiful, playful, light, fun sex that only happens between good friends. We told each other what we liked instead of making each other guess. It was the kind of sex that allows for giggling and conversation in the middle.

I liked watching Elsie and Jordan together. When they touched each other, my own skin prickled as if I was being touched. Her legs were thick and strong and so soft at the same time. She was quiet at first, and I paid attention to how her breathing changed as I tried different kinds of touch. Her legs trembled when I hit the right spot, and I felt my own body tremble. We all came at the same time, and then broke down in hysterical laughter.

We held each other in Elsie's bed for a while until Jordan started to yawn. He and I got dressed.

Elsie reached from the bed over to a chair where we'd draped her dress. I told her not to get up, to revel in the afterglow. I wanted to remember this picture of her, relaxed and happy and unconcerned.

We slept together one more time after that, but a week later Elsie came over to our place to hang out and told us her boyfriend was having a hard time with jealousy. She said we had to stop sleeping together. We hugged each other and promised to hike together again soon.

Once Elsie left, Jordan slumped into a chair. "I hadn't expected this to feel like a breakup, but it does," he said. He rubbed his face with his hands. "I feel rejected."

"Oh, honey." I hugged him. "It was really good while it lasted. But our friendship is more important to me than a romantic relationship." I didn't admit I felt sad and stung. "Who knows, maybe if we handle this gracefully, we'll be able to see each other romantically again someday." Though from what Elsie had shared about her partner's reaction, I had a hunch we wouldn't get back to where we'd been.

"It will feel better with a little time," I told Jordan.

12

Too Eager for Intimacy

"*You.* I want to see you naked."

I heard a woman's voice ring out with this sentence from across the party, and I looked up to see Rachel pointing directly at me. She was the hostess of this party, and she'd led the way down the street to a secret inlet of the lake. People were skinny-dipping, their bodies steely in the moonlight, and she wanted me to join in.

It was a hot, sticky August night in Austin, where I was traveling for work. I'd left teaching for a dream job working mostly remotely for a book publisher, and I was back and forth between Tucson and Austin so often that I'd begun to think of this stretch of East Sixth Street as my neighborhood.

The two bars I could see from my short-term apartment window stayed loud and rowdy until eleven at night. Even with earplugs and an eye shade I couldn't sleep, and living there part-time, I couldn't afford a quieter place. Most nights I joined the shouting crowd, listened to music, and flirted with strangers. That's where I'd met a guy who'd invited me to Rachel's party out by Lady Bird Lake.

I hadn't met Rachel before this party, and I'd barely said hi to her before this moment. She was adorable, her long bangs almost covering her eyes, auburn hair waving down to her waist, half a dozen thin chain necklaces draping down her chest that she stroked with her fingertips.

When this unabashed force of a woman wanted me to take my clothes off, my ego took a *biiiiig* fucking victory lap around my mind. I felt so confident that when Radio K told me to suck in my belly as I pulled my shirt over my head, I told him to fuck off.

No one knew me in Austin, and I felt bold in the anonymity at first. I experimented with telling strangers that my boyfriend was nine hundred miles away and had given me a hall pass, and the reaction thrilled me every time. Their eyebrows would lift, and then their eyes would flick down my body and back up.

With a sentence I became an exciting puzzle. People wanted to know how Jordan and I opened our relationship, how we talked about our dates, how we dealt with jealousy. But though I spent a lot of time talking about dating around, I didn't actually have the confidence to ask anyone out on dates.

So I created a forcing function for myself. I drank.

For example, when I was out to dinner with my bubbly bi friend May, we both talked about how hard it was to flirt with girls, because girls make such easy friends, and you can never tell if they're leaning in to tell you a secret or leaning in to kiss you. We talked about these things while leaning in toward each other, our hands just millimeters from each other's thighs.

I was pretty sure May was flirting with me, and I *really* wanted to kiss her. It would have felt sexy to brazenly ask if she was flirting with me. To lean in, put my lips against her hair, and ask if I could kiss her. To tell her I liked her and that it would be totally fine with me if she wanted to just stay friends, but I'd think it was awesome if she wanted to be more. To close that millimeter gap and let my fingertips touch her thigh.

Instead, I opened my mouth to pour more wine down my throat. The first glass of wine went down just to calm my nerves. My stomach was fluttering and jumping, so I didn't eat much. I ordered another glass because I like the taste of wine, I told myself, and because maybe if I relaxed a little more, I'd just say the things I was thinking. Instead, the second glass made my tongue thick and loose at the same time. My tongue was uncontrollable, and not in the way that helped me tell the truth but in the way that garbled and slurred the truth.

I smiled, stood up, and announced I was going to the bathroom. I'd be back in a sec. The hall leading to the bathroom was narrow, and I dragged my finger along the wall to steady my swaying.

I retched in the toilet. Forcing function failed.

This was my pattern for a while. Go out for drinks with a hot new friend, get too drunk because I wanted to kiss her, vomit, and pledge not to try to kiss her with my vomit breath. I kept Altoids in my purse.

When I met Rachel, I'd already noticed my binge-drinking-for-confidence pattern. I wasn't drinking at the lake. So when Rachel pointed at me across the party, I knew it wasn't drunken charm that had done me any favors. She just liked *me*. I loved how direct she was about it—more direct than I'd yet been able to be with anyone I liked about what I wanted.

We waited out the party, past midnight, then one, then two. One by one everyone left, until it was just her and me. The tequila on her lips was sharp and bright.

We'd been sitting on a rock at the edge of the water, and Rachel slid down onto the grass and took hold of my legs to position herself between them. She wrapped her arms around my hips. And then her mouth was on me.

Immediately, I didn't like it. Suddenly the lust-magic of the moment broke for me, and I looked at the horizon to see if the sky was starting to lighten. Everything was a flat, dull gray in the moonlight. How long had we been out here? I started to get restless. I started to hope I would come fast. Which of course never happens when you're trying to make it happen.

Rachel suddenly looked up. "What do you like?" she asked.

All the times I'd been asked this question in my life, I got so awkward trying to respond that I shut down. I never knew how to answer. I'd decided at some point that it was enough to say I didn't know what I liked until I felt it, and to leave it at that.

But I wanted to answer Rachel differently. This girl was direct, and blunt, and I liked that, and I suddenly felt emboldened to try being that way. I leaned forward and looked her in the eye. In a low, soft voice I said, "I like long, slow, light licks at first. Tease me."

She did. And it was amazing. The lines she traced with her tongue sent a ripple of goosebumps up my spine and along my ribs and shoulders. When I wanted her to go faster, I told her so. I came in just a couple of minutes.

I told her I wanted to return the favor, and we switched positions. I felt her thighs, her hips, her waist. I ran my mouth from her inner knee to her pubic bone. And then, taking a page from her book, I asked what she liked, and buried my mouth in her belly as I looked up at her.

She stiffened. Then froze. Her face twisted.

"I don't know," she said.

"That's okay. I'll experiment," I said, but Rachel wriggled away from my hands and reached for a pack of cigarettes. She clicked the lighter desperately about seven times until a flame finally popped out. Her fingers were shaking, even worse after she took a drag. Her head lolled a little in a tequila haze.

"I can't orgasm with Max," she said. Her boyfriend. "Do you know what that's like?"

I shook my head. "I mean, I've been frustrated before—" I should have kept my mouth shut. It was a stupid thing to say.

"No, that's not the same. You don't know what it's like."

I shook my head. "You're right. It's not the same."

"I've actually never orgasmed with a partner, only when I'm alone." She looked left and right until she spotted the bottle of tequila just within reach at the base of a tree. She took a pull. "I don't fucking know what I like."

"I'm sorry," I said. Another stupid thing.

"Yeah," she said, a bite of sarcasm in her voice.

"Do you want to go inside?"

I'm not even entirely sure Rachel heard my question. She was lost in thought, taking drags from her cigarette, holding her knees closed with her other hand.

"I just want to feel what that's like, you know?" she whispered.

"I'm happy to try," I said, smiling. But she shook her head.

"It feels awkward and terrible when it doesn't happen."

"I don't mind," I said. Which I meant to be encouraging. But.

"*I* do," she snapped, and turned her head away, toward the road.

I pulled up onto the rock and sat next to her. She took another drag of her cigarette, and she didn't look back at me.

I wish I'd told her I knew what it was like to not know what you liked or wanted. I wish I'd told her how courageous I felt around her, that I felt like I'd gotten to borrow some of her confidence that night. I wanted to reflect her own assertiveness back to her.

But I didn't say those things. Rachel seemed trapped in a spell. She turned her head partway back to me, but she still didn't look me in the eye. She stared blankly into the water and sighed heavily.

I smelled tequila, and I felt blank too. And cold. I couldn't think of anything to say that could break this feeling.

"It's really late," I said. "Let's go back inside and you can get some sleep."

Rachel didn't move. Smoke from her cigarette wafted into her eyes, and she blinked to clear it away, but she didn't move the hand holding the cigarette.

I didn't move either. I breathed in deep, leaned back on my hands, and looked up at the stars overhead. An old part of me wanted to grab a towel and get us both clothed and back inside so we could reset.

But a new part of me realized that I didn't need to rush through this moment. It takes time and quiet to feel. I let myself let go of feeling embarrassed for being naked, for having sex with a girl I'd just met that night. I let go of wanting to say something that would fix things for Rachel, as if that was possible for a stranger to do in an instant.

We just sat there together, breathing. Rachel stopped taking drags of her cigarette. When it burned down to the filter, she stubbed it out on the rock, stood up, and slowly walked to the tree where she'd tossed her towel.

"I'm cold," she said.

I nodded and got up just as slowly. I was mostly dry already, and I pulled on my clothes. Rachel just wadded her clothes up in her fist and wrapped the towel tightly around herself. I picked up the bottle of tequila.

We walked silently back to her house, where I set the tequila bottle down on the counter. "Sleep well," I said, and we hugged and held on for a few beats. She filled up a glass of water and went toward her bedroom, and I shut the door behind me.

Outside, the horizon was turning pale. My stomach turned for a moment, thinking of how little sleep I was going to get, but then I felt okay. All I needed was a little time.

13

Pick Me

Jordan and I got on dating apps because, first of all, they didn't exist when we first got together, so they were a new, exciting way to check out the dating pool, and second, it's thrilling to get attention from strangers.

I didn't even care that the premise of dating apps is objectifying; I *liked* them because they were objectifying. I liked that some sliver of me could be compelling enough for someone to choose me out of a running list of possibilities. I liked that strangers would only see the parts of me I wanted them to see.

I could show them my playfulness and wit, but I could hold back my neuroses. I could post a photo in a short skirt, subtly flexing my quadriceps, and they would see my defined thighs but not the chub on my knees. I liked the idea that I got to curate my most flirtatious version of myself, and some stranger might look at it and swipe their thumb across my face, thinking, *Her. I want to see her naked. I want to try to make her laugh.*

But for the very reasons I liked the idea of a dating profile, I felt wildly uncertain while I was writing it. It felt like a big effort to hide the parts of myself I was sure would poke through: my awkwardness, my insecurity, my gullibility. I tried to smooth it all over with a veneer of cool.

In the "About me" section, I wrote: *Professional word wrestler who likes old fashioneds and blues singers who belt their hearts out.*

Translation: Insecure poser who may or may not actually make a living as a writer.

It wasn't like I loved blues. I just loved performers who could emote so easily, when it took me so many drafts to spell out what I thought and felt.

My photos included an impromptu shot my friend had taken of me in New York, wearing a sexy cowl neck dress in a stairwell lit by Edison bulbs; a photo of Jordan and me overlooking a beautiful stretch of wilderness; me pointing at the Grand Canyon like I'd discovered it; and—oh god, I'm remembering with agony—a picture of me straddling my friend's vintage motorcycle, in a short, patterned sundress and fancy flip-flops. I was not going anywhere on that bike, which was almost too heavy for me to even lift from its stand.

Seriously? Who is this girl?

You don't even know, do you? Radio K added.

I struggled to describe myself because I was a chameleon. I wanted people to like me so much that I faked myself into being whomever they wanted me to be.

I'm a girl who wants someone to pick me out of a crowd and tell me who I am.

But I didn't write that.

To cut my profile off at the neck, I wrote at the bottom, under the "Who are you seeking?" section: *I'm looking primarily to build close friendships. If they go somewhere else, cool.*

That line was bullshit, but I didn't let myself see that at the time. It was true that I was trying to create close friendships in my life. My two best friends had moved to different cities months before, and I was devastated. But that's why I'd started going to dance classes. It didn't explain why I was on OkCupid.

The next line was slightly more honest: *I'm interested in pursuing a relationship with a woman if things click.*

And the last line was bolder: *My boyfriend and I are open to seeing someone together if the fit is right.*

I felt weird writing that last line. I thought back to a night with Zadie, a few months after she'd left her husband to date women. We'd had a couple of sidecars together, sitting in a dark corner booth of our favorite bar, and she'd bitched about how many of the women on dating apps who posted they were "seeking women" turned out to be straight girls in disguise. She didn't want to be someone's experimental hookup, she'd said. And she was skeeved out by the "unicorn hunters," the term she used for couples who wanted a third to guest star in their sex life.

If Zadie had seen my profile, she would have swiped left, no question. I hated the idea that if Zadie and I were strangers, she would despise me as much as she despised the rest of the unicorn hunters.

In the year or so since Jordan and I had opened our relationship, I'd wondered whether I would want to be in a relationship with a woman. I found women gorgeous, and I craved close connections to women in my friendships, but a romantic relationship was different, surely. *Could I even be romantically attracted to a woman?* the heterosexually conditioned part of my brain asked.

You already are, whispered a quieter, calmer part of me. *Welcome home to yourself.*

* * *

The first woman I met for a date was Josephine. We went to a gelateria in Austin. After five minutes of casting about for topics we were both interested in, we realized we had nothing in common. Josephine was really into manga and anime; I'd never heard of any of the characters she mentioned. I asked if she liked to hike, but she said she'd rather spend a whole day deep in video games. I shuddered, thinking back to my ex, Sam, on the couch playing endless video games and never looking up.

"I was *so* into Zelda as a kid," Josephine said. "I wanted to be her."

"Everyone wanted to be her," I sympathized, though I couldn't remember if I'd ever played the game.

Josephine stabbed her tiny spoon into her gelato, set it down, and looked at me slightly sideways. "Are you interested in dating me?" she asked.

My cheeks flushed with panic at being put on the spot. I admired her guts to be direct, but I couldn't bring myself to respond as directly. My tongue felt full of lead.

"I think you're attractive," I said, "but I don't feel a spark. I'd like to be friends. I wanted to meet you because you wrote in your profile you were working on a novel, and I'm looking for writing partners. What's your novel about?"

In a bored voice, Josephine described her complex, *Star Wars*-like plot involving characters who lived in floating colonies in the atmosphere of a far-flung planet. When she was done, she gave me that hard, sideways look again for a moment, and then she took a breath and seemed to relax.

"Can I ask you a question?" she asked.

"Sure," I said, trying to busy myself scraping the last dregs of gelato out of my cup.

"Do I pass easily?"

I knew what she meant. In her dating profile, she hadn't directly said she was trans, but her title read "Josephine (not Joseph)."

I smiled and scanned her face. Her black hair fell just past her collar bones, and her perfect straight bangs traced a line just above her neatly plucked eyebrows. She had a long fine nose and almond eyes. She was beautiful. "Definitely," I said.

Josephine leaned back in her chair, and her shoulders relaxed. "I thought so, but I still worry about it. Sometimes friends post old photos of me from before I transitioned, and it's still a gut punch every time I get surprised with a picture of my old self. Do you know how to take a tag off when someone's tagged you on social media?"

I shook my head. "Sorry," I said. "God, that's rough."

"I know people don't do it to be mean, but it's really triggering to me," she said.

"I'm sure."

"And I've always been into women, but I've never known how to approach women. I thought it would be easier when I looked the way I wanted, but it's just more confusing. How can you tell when they're into you romantically versus just being into you as a friend?"

I chuckled. "I wish I could tell you. I have no idea. You did a good job asking, though. I really admire that."

"But you're not into me."

I shrugged. "I'm not a gamer."

"I thought there would be a secret Sapphic handshake or something," Josephine joked. "Or I thought maybe there would be some way women touch each other when they're dating—"

"—but women friends touch each other all the time," I finished for her. "I know! It's really confusing."

"Damn," Josephine said. "I was really hoping you could at least help me with *that*."

We both stood up, threw away our cups, and shook hands. "Sorry to disappoint," I said. "But send me your novel. I'd love to read it."

Josephine agreed, and we parted ways. A few days later, she emailed me her novel. It was really good. She didn't want to meet up to talk more about it, though.

*   *   *

I had another date with a woman in Tucson who seemed cool on paper: she was a cyclist and a journalist, and when we met, she looked nervous as hell. Or she just instantly didn't like me. When we identified each other at the café, she forced a smile that I didn't see return throughout our lunch date.

I suddenly became very aware of how often I look people in the eye, because she would only meet my gaze for a fraction of a second before her eyes darted somewhere else around the room. I ordered a Cubano, and she told me she was vegetarian because she couldn't stomach animal cruelty. And here's the thing—I *really* like food. So when my sandwich came and I started munching on the probably-tortured dead pig in my hands, I tried and failed to suppress my pleasure. My date looked horrified.

I asked about her newspaper job, and it turned out she hated it—and hated writing. I asked her about cycling and she described it less as a passion and more as a self-inflicted penance of some kind. Midway through my sandwich I thought, *Why am I trying so hard to engage this girl?*

A small, tender voice piped up. *You want her to feel comfortable, and you want her to like you. But you can't control how she feels.*

Nah, the problem is you can't stand being disliked by anyone, Radio K countered. *You want to be universally adored. Her disinterest proves you are not.*

I was about to dive straight into an anxiety spiral about how self-centered I was when the small, tender voice came back. *You can let go of this one.* I felt my shoulders relax.

We ran out of things to talk about, and I realized I didn't care. I munched happily on the last few bites of my sandwich. She finished before me, and as soon as I was done, she stood up and wished me a good afternoon.

We gave each other a one-armed hug. I never heard from her again, and for the first time, I walked away without wondering what she thought of me.

. . .

Then there was the unicorn—the blessed, beautiful, mature twenty-something with gorgeously full lips who wanted to date Jordan and me both. We went out to brunch and clicked, especially she and Jordan, who both have a sarcastic streak. They traded *Simpsons* references that flew over my head. We all got a little day-drunk. We saw each other several times after that, but I choked at every moment I could have taken the leap to ask if she wanted to play. Jordan never leapt because he thought it would be better for me to initiate.

Later, after she started dating someone else and we'd settled into a friendship, she bemoaned how obviously she'd tried to flirt with me and how I never seemed to catch on. I'd spent all our interactions worrying that she would feel weirded out if I asked her to bed with us. I caught the small moments when she teased me or Jordan, but they never seemed enthusiastic enough to overcome my paranoia.

I still believed that I wasn't normal for wanting threesomes. I was afraid that she might get upset if I propositioned her, and she would take all the shame I'd been holding in my head and throw it in my face.

So no one made a move, and she started dating a guy who was not interested in nonmonogamy and didn't want to meet her new friends who wanted to fuck her. I can't imagine why.

Then I met Christine, the first woman I let myself fall in love with. Codependently and crushingly.

14

Here's Why They Call It a Crush

I'm only just now starting to understand that other people don't necessarily have everything more figured out than me.

But for a long time, I trusted that other people, with their outside perspectives, had a better handle on the world. Other people always seemed to pick up details about the world that I missed because I was consumed by my self-critical inner dialogue. I wrongly assumed that someone else's vision would always be better at cutting through the noise in my head to see me for who I am.

To give just one example of how stupid this gets sometimes, I went to a Chinese medicine guy for a while who does tui-na massage, and in our first session, he had just hit a tight spot on my IT band when he suddenly said, "Do you usually wear glasses?"

I was face down on the table, and I turned to look back at him and said, "*Wait*—can you tell that from the tightness in my IT band or something?"

He chuckled. "No, I just think I've seen you at the coffee shop before."

So…yeah. I thought other people were magic. It's taken me a long time to realize that no one can understand me better than I understand myself.

* * *

I instantly withered in Christine's presence. I went to that first date with her feeling pretty put-together: I had a stable long-term relationship; Jordan and I were tiptoeing up to a decade together. I loved my job and it paid well. I traveled a lot on adventures. I'd worn a dress that I thought rode a good line between sexy and cute, and I wasn't so dolled up that I felt fake. I felt remarkably self-assured, considering the mental chatter I was usually working with.

She chose our meeting spot, a sushi bar in downtown Austin I hadn't yet visited because of its hefty price tag. Christine walked up to the restaurant, somehow looking feminine, professional, and a little punk rock all at once in a black collared jumpsuit that tapered mid-shin and black lace-up boots. Her silver-blond hair was in a close-cropped pixie cut that looked playful and effortlessly striking at the same time.

She was about my height, but I suddenly felt smaller and child-ish. As she walked closer, I couldn't decide whether to hug her or shake her hand, and at the last moment I defaulted to an awkward side hug.

She ordered a martini to start and even gave the bartender custom directions on how she wanted it made. Up to that point, I had thought martinis were disgusting (seriously, who likes a flavor profile that combines *salty* with *medicinal?*), but I told the bartender to make me one too. Not because I wanted a martini, but because I wanted to be *that cool.*

Within the first few minutes of get-to-know-you conversation, Christine said that she was a lawyer and very good at reading tiny details on people's faces and in their gestures. Just from someone's posture or how fast they spoke, she could tell when people were freaking out inside and calling out for help or when they were lying. And sitting across from her, nervous as hell, I just thought:

Can she see the shit I'm trying not to show her? Has she noticed that I'm swallowing a lot, and will she see that my lips are sometimes slightly sticking together because my mouth is so dry? Am I staring too intensely? Do I look relaxed? Or are my shoulders weirdly rigid? I want her to think I have an athletic posture. Am I leaning too far forward on the table? Oh my god my ears are ringing can she tell I'm only half paying attention to what she's saying?

I was sure Christine could see right through me, and I admired her for it. I wanted to learn how to be like her.

Christine and I ate sushi, which was difficult to take small bites of. I tried not to chew with my mouth open, which meant I sometimes had to swallow balls of rice whole and just cross my fingers that I wouldn't choke. I tried to keep my arms off the table. I tried not to hunch, and mentally rehearsed the table manners I'd been taught as a kid, back when I'd be made to stand up at the table to eat if I scraped my fork against my teeth. I tried to sip my martini slowly and hoped Christine couldn't somehow read in my eyes that I really wanted to slam my drink back so I could stop the dual chatter in my head as Radio K and my father went at it about the best way to make oneself look respectable at the dinner table.

By the time we finished dinner, I was simultaneously fascinated by Christine and utterly convinced I wasn't cool enough, mature enough, observant enough, or interesting enough for her. I hadn't made her laugh once.

We said goodbye, looking each other straight in the eyes, and then she walked away to her car. I leaned against the brick wall for a minute, hating my own indecision. *Would it have killed me to just open my mouth and ask if she wanted to make out?*

I saw her get in her car; it wasn't the sleek sedan I would have expected, but a decades-old Bronco with rust damage on the back fender. Somehow it made her seem more approachable, more down to earth. I sent a text:

I really wish I'd kissed you just now.

Christine's Bronco pulled away, turned the corner, and was gone.

A minute later she replied that next time I could make it up to her.

My palms were sweaty the whole ride back to my rented room.

*   *   *

At the end of our second date, as I walked her to her car, her text flashed in my mind. My hands and legs suddenly felt jittery, and my breath got rapid and shallow.

Before Christine could pull out her keys, I took her by the hips and pressed her against the side of her car. For just a moment I felt like a teenager: impulsive, unsure, immature. My neck twitched and I shoved the thought aside. Then I reached for the back of her neck and pulled her mouth to mine.

We made out under the streetlight for several minutes before the back door of the restaurant opened and a busboy came out with a bag of trash and a jingling crate of bottles. Christine pulled back for a second, but she didn't break her gaze. She just giggled at the clanking of the busboy chucking everything into the dumpster, and kissed me again. I played with the short hem of her dress.

From that moment on I was, in a word, besotted.

15

When I'm Found,
I Want to Hide

Instead of going out for our next date, Christine brought a bottle of whiskey to my place, which was really Deb's place. I'd met Deb on one of my first trips to Austin, and she let me rent her guest room for weeks at a time for next to nothing. I introduced Christine to Deb, and Christine cracked the bottle of whiskey and poured each of us a drink. Deb took hers into her bedroom, shooting me a half-raised eyebrow on her way out. Christine and I took our tumblers and the bottle to my room.

My skin was trembling. There was nothing interesting in the guest room, just a futon bed and a child's dresser left over from Deb's niece who sometimes stayed there. There were no board games stashed away, no TV. I sat on the edge of the futon and looked up at Christine. I scrambled for something to ask her about herself. I knew the only interesting thing we could do in this room was talk or have sex, and I was so nervous, my mind went completely blank.

I took a sip of whiskey and asked if she'd seen some show I'd been recently binge-watching. Christine didn't answer. She smiled, took a sip from her glass, and set it on top of the dresser. Then she leaned over and put her hands on my thighs.

"I'm more interested in you right now," she said in a silky voice.

Christine kissed me and pulled up the edges of my shirt. I kicked myself for wearing a pullover bra, even if it was lacy. Christine tried to pull it up, but it got stuck on my shoulders and I leaned back and pulled it off myself. It was not the most glamorous first view of my naked boobs.

But when I sat up, Christine had knelt down and was just looking at me. Her eyes traced my breasts, my neck, my face, and finally met my eyes again. My whole body felt hot with embarrassment and excitement. I loved the way she looked at me, and I also felt agitated. I couldn't sit still.

I grabbed the waist of her pants and pulled her closer until she couldn't see all of me. I pulled her shirt off. I held the back of her neck with one hand and I fiddled with the clasp of her bra with the other. I couldn't get it undone, and I swore at myself in my head. I hadn't even thought to practice this; I could get my own bra off with one hand behind my back. *Why the fuck won't it come undone?*

Christine kneeled upright and brought both hands back to unhook her bra. Then she pulled my shorts and underwear down. I reached for her again, trying to pull her in close so she couldn't look at me, but she sat back on her heels. She put her hands on my legs and separated my knees.

"I just want to look at you," she said.

My throat got tight as I thought about how the small soft chub on my stomach probably poked out from the angle she saw me from. I leaned back on my forearms and sucked in my stomach slightly. Christine pushed her hands up my thighs until she was holding my hips, until she was using her thumbs to trace my vulva. I swallowed and tried to take deeper breaths as I watched her.

* * *

Jordan had looked at me this closely before, but he knew how deeply insecure I was about it, and he always thought of playful ways to approach me. I never had trouble relaxing during oral sex, but when he just wanted to look at me, I always closed my legs or pulled him up closer to me. I thought my vulva looked weird, and I thought my butt and thighs must look awkward from that vantage point.

Jordan kissed my thighs and teased me that he wanted to run a science experiment, so I needed to hold still. He ran his fingers up my thighs and tickled my hip creases. When I giggled and kicked, he told me to hold still again. He muttered to himself as if he were a scientist noting his observations. "Displays a kicking reflex when palpated at the hip flexors."

As he explored me with his fingers, he noted my reaction moment by moment. I laughed at the first few, and then I started to loosen up and relax. "Moans when I apply pressure," Jordan said, and I told him to shut up and just keep doing whatever he was doing.

. . .

Christine didn't let me shy away into humor. She didn't let me pull her up. She looked at me, occasionally flicking her eyes up to see if I was watching. I was. She cocked her head to one side, studying me.

She propped herself up on one elbow, one hand supporting her neck as she used the other hand to trace my labia. Her movements were more sincere than sexy, and I trembled under her gaze.

Excitement rolled through me in big waves, each one followed immediately by a crash of shame. *Just breathe,* the tender voice in my head whispered. *This is what it looks like when you start letting go of your shame. It follows your excitement around for a while, trying to pull you back from letting go too much. You're starting to notice. That's all you need to do for now.*

I closed my eyes and threw my head back, letting myself concentrate on the incredible sensations I felt at her fingertips. I pulled a pillow over my face to muffle my moans.

After I came, she slid up next to me. "That was so beautiful," she said, and nuzzled into my neck. I felt beautiful. I felt overwhelmed with pleasure and inhibition and freedom all at the same time. My head throbbed. I wrapped my arms around her and pressed her face into my chest.

Then I rolled her over, inched her black jeans down, and studied her.

. . .

We met up two or three nights a week when I was in Austin. It was awkward finding space to have sex. Most weeks, Christine had kids and a babysitter at home, so her place was out. Deb was a socialite and often had friends over, and I felt self-conscious with Christine in the guest room with its thin walls. Some nights Deb went out, and we had the house to ourselves, but we weren't discreet and often botched the timing.

Once, Deb came home when I was mid-orgasm on the living room couch. Christine was in a shirt and underwear, but I was naked, and when I heard Deb's key in the lock, I curled up reflexively like a pill bug. She opened the door, took one glance inside, and quickly snapped the door shut. Then she texted me: *I'll go for one more drink. Back in twenty.*

Deb is a saint, I thought as Christine and I got dressed.

On our next date, I picked Christine up at her house. After dinner we messed around in the back of her Bronco, parked on the street in front of her house. Her babysitter was inside with her two boys. She'd parked next to a wall so no one could see her car or what we were doing inside it. Afterward, she went inside to relieve the babysitter, and I walked around the block to order a ride before the babysitter came outside.

* * *

Then came the night that we didn't have sex. Instead, I came to her house, and we drank wine in her open courtyard, looking at the stars. We told each other family ghost stories. She described how, years ago, she'd felt a dark entity in her house and had performed rituals to clear it.

This all seemed strange coming from a lawyer. But I was riveted. This is what it looked like for her to trust her body over her logical mind. I was envious.

"How do you clear energy?" I asked.

Christine closed her eyes. "First I ground myself. I feel my feet in contact with the ground, and I feel gravity pulling my body down to earth. Then I imagine this pillar of light coming up through me, out the crown of my head, like a channel, and I use the channel to move the energy through."

I closed my eyes and tried to imagine what she meant. I could feel the weight of my body in the chair, and I could picture a blue light above my head, but I couldn't feel anything changing.

"I don't understand," I admitted.

"It's not something to be worked out through logic," Christine said. "There are things our brains can't take in and process on their own. I trust what my body senses, even when my brain can't explain why."

My logical mind thought these ideas sounded crazy. But the rest of me wanted to feel the kind of certainty Christine felt with herself. I wanted to trust myself that much.

•   •   •

There was one big hazard of falling in love with Christine: I felt more seen. Which made me want to hide.

In contrast to Christine's self-assuredness, I felt like a total anxiety ball. One date night, Christine and I were supposed to go to a show together, and I had something verging on a panic attack in the car. It had been a long workday; some minor problem had snowballed, and I'd gone hours without a bathroom break and had forgotten to eat lunch.

By the time Christine showed up to pick me up, my eyes were bloodshot and dry, and I felt jittery from low blood sugar. I blew off how I felt, shoved on my shoes, and got in the car without dinner.

As Christine drove, I willed myself to relax. Instead, my thoughts spiraled. *I really should have eaten something, but it's too late now. Relax; you only get a little bit of time each week with Christine, and there's no use sucking it up with your anxious bullshit. Come on, this show will be fun! Won't it? What if I start to feel anxious like I usually do around crowds and I go hide out in the bathroom but then I can't find her in the audience when I come back—YOU HAVE TO RELAX.*

Christine took one hand off the steering wheel and held my hand. She turned to look at me. "Are you okay?"

I got nervous that she didn't have her eyes on the road or both her hands on the wheel, and I just said yes. But then I started to hyperventilate.

"I'm sorry," I choked out. "I just feel really anxious."

Christine turned off the main drag onto a side street and put the car in park. "We don't have to go," she said.

"You were looking forward to this," I protested. "And we're going to be late."

Christine put her hand on my shoulder. "I don't care about the show. Let's go to your place and have some tea, okay?"

I took a big breath. "Okay." Christine turned the car around, and I instantly felt better.

I also instantly felt guilty for ruining the evening.

We sat on my bed all night, our backs leaned against the wall. Between a thousand apologies I tried to explain the flood of thoughts that were racing through my mind. She told me to slow down. I told her I couldn't; there was so much to do all the time that I always brought my phone into the bathroom with me to answer work email while I was peeing.

"You could start there, with something small," Christine said. "Leave your phone on your desk when you go to the bathroom. Just feel what it feels like to pee. Feel the physical relief that comes from accomplishing something."

"Peeing isn't accomplishing something," I said.

"Paying attention to your body is," she said. "And your body is pretty talented." She nudged my shoulder.

I felt like a child. *Do I really need a cheerleader for peeing? How is peeing without my phone in my hand supposed to fix my anxiety?*

But when I got up and went to the bathroom, I realized she was right. Relief flooded my entire body. It felt really good. And I felt calmer.

I collapsed on the couch next to her. "So much better," I said and snuggled against her chest.

I started to adopt Christine's habits. When I was unsure about something, I put my hand over my heart, closed my eyes, and let myself feel what was going on inside my body until I knew what I wanted to do. I was learning how to be stronger in my self-belief.

Because this connection to myself was so new and unfamiliar, I attributed the beauty of it to Christine. I fell in love with her.

16

Mom, Meet My
Secret Life

I'm surprised I didn't get into a car accident when I told my mom about Christine. Like any smart-but-panicking woman who wants to connect with her mother, I chose to start that conversation while we were trapped in the car. I kept my eyes glued to the road and my hands white-knuckled on the steering wheel.

By the time my mom came to visit Jordan and me in Tucson, I'd been dating Christine for six months or so, making trips to Austin every few weeks. I hadn't told either of my parents that Jordan and I had opened our relationship or that I was dating a woman. Now that I was starting to connect to myself, I realized how disconnected I'd been on phone calls with my parents.

Because I wasn't talking about Christine, I wasn't talking about a lot of my life. My connection with my parents was eroding in one tiny silence at a time. Our phone calls were bland and lifeless and mostly about the weather or what friend of theirs had gotten the flu or which of my nephews had busted a knee falling off his bike.

I kept telling myself it was the physical distance that made it hard to talk about my being queer. I didn't want to come out to my parents over the phone. I'd come close a couple of times. I'd mention "my friend Christine" and then find myself opening my mouth and taking a breath—and just as I was on the cusp of adding "Christine is also my partner, actually," Radio K would jump in, whispering through the phone, *They're going to think you're a sex-obsessed, disgusting freak.*

I was especially afraid of my dad's reaction. Once, when I was in high school, I'd asked my dad while we were all sitting down to dinner, "What would you think if I were gay?"

My dad's face froze. He said nothing.

A few beats passed before my mom leaned toward him, looked him in the eye, and said to me, "We would love you." My dad said nothing; he just grunted.

I was terrified of those silent beats that stretched between us. Of the two of them, my mom seemed more approachable on this topic.

Leading up to my mom's visit, I'd decided I wanted to tell her about my relationship. I wanted to tell her that I was into women, that Jordan was cool with it, that I was pretty sure I was in love with Christine. I imagined the conversation in my head a million times. I was just waiting for the right moment, when she and I were alone, to sit down over a glass of wine and have a heart-to-heart.

Except the right moment never came. Jordan and I were in the middle of remodeling our house, and we were always working on something together. Radio K teased me constantly throughout the day. *So, what, you're going to take a break from pulling up tile to say, "Hey Mom, I like to lick pussy now?"*

* * *

Then there was the afternoon my mom and I met two of my girlfriends for a glass of wine. It was only supposed to be an hour, honest. But there were four of us and bottles of wine were half off, so we bought a bottle of something deliriously silky that tasted of currants and leather, and my mom started laughing in that beautiful whole-faced way she does, when she opens her mouth so wide you can see her fillings.

We gabbed about some problem one of my friends was having with her boyfriend, and my mom shared her wisdom from several decades ahead of us, and then the other girlfriend in the group was supposed to go meet some guy at a local distillery. She was nervous and didn't actually want to date him, and she asked us all to come along. We could be a little safety net in the corner that she could retreat to if she wanted an easy exit.

I looked at my mom and reminded her that we had soup at home, and maybe we should call it quits. But my mom had a sweet, devilish-mischievous look in her eye, and she said she wasn't hungry yet. "Let's just go, and we'll stay for a little while, and *then* we'll go home for dinner."

Just to frame how sweet an offer this was: I've never seen my mother drink hard alcohol without wincing and pushing the glass away. She wasn't interested at all in a distillery. She just loved my friends that much, and loved me that much, and we were all kind of invested in the drama of this date that shouldn't even be happening.

My mom and one of the girlfriends and I sat at a booth and sipped gin and tonics (my mom between minuscule winces) while the other friend went to meet the guy up at the bar. At one point the guy came over to introduce himself to us. He seemed to get kind of skittish, and then he left the bar altogether, which surprised none of us. I looked at my phone and saw it was *ten freaking o'clock* and we hadn't eaten dinner.

My mom and I both just looked at each other and dissolved into gin-infused giggles.

"I forgot to feed you!" I joked.

It wasn't just a joke, though. I felt guilty for getting caught up in my friends, caught up in the moment, and not stopping to think about what she needed. Never mind that my mother was an adult who could take care of what she needed; that thought didn't cross my mind.

My mom shook her head. "There's nowhere I'd rather be."

We walked to the bougie downtown market and wandered through, looking for anything that appealed to our hunger on a hot Tucson end-of-summer night. There was a hot bar full of all kinds of slow-cooked, herb-infused foods, but we were having none of it.

Instead, we wandered over to the refrigerator aisle, mostly to open the doors and cool ourselves off a little bit. That night, my mother and I ate yogurt for dinner at ten at night and I got her home a good four hours past her bedtime.

. . .

As I was trying to fall asleep, I agonized over why I hadn't told her about Christine that night. I'd thought about it several times. There was a moment when one of my friends was with the awkward date and the other friend had gone to the bathroom, and I almost blurted it out then. My mom seemed so happy and ready for anything; it was the perfect opportunity to tell her the truth. But I didn't want anything to break the spell.

That night I had this dream where a friend of mine, Dylan, came out to me as gay. He was about to tell his parents. We had a heart-to-heart about what he'd been afraid of. Dylan said he was scared to tell any of us because he didn't want us to look at him differently. He worried we'd stop talking to him. That we wouldn't accept the people in his life whom he loved. That we'd think we never really knew him at all.

In the dream, I felt so sad that he'd worried *I* would think those things or that I would be awkward or dismissive or cold toward him. I felt so much closer to him, and I was happy he didn't have to fake anything anymore.

And then, the dream skipped ahead to after Dylan told his parents, and he came back to me beaming. He was glowing all over in gold light, and he was so happy. He said he felt free. He could actually be himself now and let people in for real. I felt so happy for him, and so proud. I told him I thought it was one of the bravest things I'd ever seen anyone do.

All the people in your dreams are you.

When I woke up, I realized I had to tell my mom.

. . .

The moment I picked was not ideal. We were driving back from the home improvement store. I picked this moment not because it was the right one, but because it might be the last one. She and I were alone for the first time, and she was leaving the next day. Plus, we were both trapped in a moving vehicle, so that's pretty convenient.

I just spilled it out all at once in a rush. "There's something I've been wanting to tell you, and it's weird to talk about...Jordan and I have an open relationship, and I'm queer, and I'm dating a woman."

Smooth, right? I particularly enjoy how I prefaced it with *this is weird*—that's an important frame to set the tone apart from *this is normal* or even *this is an exciting part of myself I want to share with you*.

I don't like to turn my head to look at passengers while I'm driving, especially when I've dumped a load of emotionally charged information onto someone. I looked straight ahead, and in my periphery I saw nothing, no movement from my mom. She sat there with her hands in her lap. For several seconds, I listened to the creak of the back door panel on my van as we drove over potholes.

Finally, I couldn't take the silence anymore. "Do you have any questions?"

There we go, Radio K snickered. *Nice way to open the floor and make her feel welcome to talk. I'm sure she doesn't feel put on the spot whatsoever.*

After a few more seconds of door creaking, my mom asked, "Is Jordan dating someone else too?"

"Yes." I looked over at her. She was looking ahead.

"How do you...do that without getting emotionally involved?"

My jaw dropped. I kept driving, mouth partially open. My mind spun as I tried fill in the blank. *I don't,* I wanted to say. *I love her.* But I completely froze.

This is what happens when you tell people you're queer, Radio K teased. *All they can think about is you having sex. Now your mother thinks you're a confused, callous slut.*

Maybe she didn't think that. But I thought that about myself.

All this focus on sex, and my libido has taken a nosedive, I thought. In the months since Christine and I had started dating, I'd started shying away from sex. I felt sexy back when sex was compartmentalized. Now that our connection was growing into a real relationship, the compartments were breaking down. I had to accept that I was sexy *and* sincere, flirty *and* unsure, powerful *and* vulnerable. Not all those parts of me felt like they went together yet. *You feel slutty sometimes because you're a slut,* Radio K said. *Even your mother thinks so.*

You are so much more, a quiet voice piped up. *You love Christine. You can help your mom understand.*

"I'm...that's not the point," I said to my mom. "I'm not just having sex with her. I'm in a relationship with her. We care about each other." The steering wheel was getting sticky from my sweaty palms.

"I just don't think I could do that," my mom said.

My whole body flooded with shame. It pooled into a sour feeling in my stomach. I didn't register at the time that she'd made my share about herself, her own reaction, her own capacity. I doubted myself instead. *I don't know if I can do it either,* I thought. *I don't know if I can hold all these parts of me together.*

I felt angry and hurt and nauseous, and I withered. I didn't say anything more. I didn't know why I wanted more than one partner in my life. I wanted her to accept me and help me understand myself.

I just don't think I could do that. Her words reverberated around in my head, and I completely shut down. I felt numb as I pulled into the driveway in silence. My arms moved in robotic jerks as I put the car in park and shut off the engine.

"What's her name?" my mom asked quietly.

I let out the breath I was holding in. This question at least had a straightforward answer.

"Christine."

My playlist, which had sounded like white noise to me leading up to that moment, suddenly kicked on "Songbird" by Fleetwood Mac. I love this song. I love the scene in the show *Glee* when the popular cheerleader sings this song to her girlfriend and outs herself to the class. The song playing over the stereo felt like a code.

"Like Christine McVie," my mom said. I nodded, hoping she was making a positive association with the vinyl albums we'd listened to together, dancing in the basement when I was growing up.

My heart started to pound. We had about three seconds to end this conversation before Jordan came out to help us unload the van.

"I hope to meet her someday," my mom said quietly. I didn't turn my head to see what her face looked like.

17

In Which I Make Rash Decisions

Christine had a half-smile on one side of her mouth, the look I thought meant she wanted to have sex, and I yawned. It started as a small yawn, but I didn't try to stifle it, and my mouth opened embarrassingly wide. My eyes watered.

"I'm so tired," I said before she reached over for me. "I've been dragging all week. Maybe I'm coming down with something."

The half-smile disappeared, and Christine pinched her lips, just slightly.

"I should go home and get some sleep." I stood up. It was nine o'clock, far earlier than our dates usually ended. I really did feel tired; that was true. Christine was the one who'd told me to pay attention to my body, after all, but now that I was watching, I realized I felt tired all the time.

Love felt so big and overwhelming, and in my brain and body the overwhelm had found a hitching post: sex. Every touch felt too intense. I started to get in my own head and analyze with each kiss, *Does my body want this?*

I'm just in a slump, I thought as I got in the car. *It will pass.*

It didn't pass. I'd started to avoid Jordan's touch too. I tried to disguise my avoidance by sending suggestive texts with eggplants and peaches. I shaved my legs. I plucked my eyebrows, applied lotion, wore lacy underwear—I primped in all the ways you're supposed to, and instead of feeling sexy, I kept thinking, *Geez this is a lot of work. Why does anyone bother with all this ever?* I tried masturbating because I'd read in Mary Roach's science-y book *Bonk* that orgasms beget more orgasms, but my wanking didn't feel sensual so much as frustrating.

I was starting to feel like sex had been a hobby that I got really into for a while, and then the magic faded, and I just wanted to get the sexual release part over quickly so I could spend my time doing other things.

I can see now that what was really going on was that I was loved by two people, and I didn't feel I deserved it, and I was starting to lose my shit because of that.

Am I enough for Jordan? Am I enough for Christine? I don't feel like I'm enough for myself most of the time. I struggle so much to give myself love. There's no way I could give the love either of them needs. Christine gives me that look like she's so excited by me, but I just end up feeling like she's trying to pump me up. I feel fake trying to match her excitement. Jordan is so tender with me when I pull away from his caresses, but surely he'll get tired of my tiredness. I feel so overwhelmed. I shouldn't be feeling any of this.

Because I felt so vulnerable, I never asked Jordan or Christine how they felt when I pulled away.

I let the stories I told myself stand in for the truth I was too nervous to ask about.

I even let the stories I told myself stand in for the truth of my own emotions, which I refused to feel.

When I did have sex with Jordan or with Christine, it was beautiful and connective and intense, and I felt all the more guilty for the times I wanted to avoid it. After Jordan and I made love one night, I lay in bed, exhausted and relaxed, wondering, *Why am I resisting this?*

You're afraid to let them in, the quiet voice crept in. *The more people see of you, the more you resist being seen. You're afraid they'll find the ugly parts—the anger, the selfishness, the shame—and then they won't love you anymore. You're afraid you're not worth enough to make up for your shadow.*

You are fighting against feeling all of yourself.

I tried to manage every aspect of myself, which meant being sexy, sweet, accommodating, and understanding. It meant never being angry, rigid, cold, or impatient. But I was all those things. And I farted. I also had way too much mucus gumming up my throat, and most days I had to find a way to hock a loogie into the sink while no one was listening.

Don't get too close, or you'll see it's all a ruse.

The pillowcase smelled like my unwashed hair. My skin, so warm and cozy a few minutes ago, suddenly felt sticky and clammy. I got up to shower.

Radio K sat in the back of my brain, filing his nails and saying in that relaxed, snarky voice, *Good thing you've got two people roped up in this disaster of a sex drive.* Because I was tired and confused, I let him have the last say.

When I came back from my shower, Jordan's eyes followed my naked body as I got a T-shirt and sleep shorts out of the dresser. I felt a flash of anger. *Sometimes I want my body to just be mine.* I pulled the shorts on quickly and got frustrated when the shirt got scrunched up around my armpits.

"Awwww," Jordan said as I pulled the shirt down over my boobs. "You're putting them away."

I clenched my jaw. Then I took a breath. *Don't you want him to admire your body? Stop feeling angry.*

"Sorry," I said, as if it were my fault he was disappointed. "When I try to sleep naked, I always have anxiety dreams that I'm showing up naked in public."

Stop feeling angry. I swallowed, pulled back the covers, and got into bed. Then I scooted over and gave Jordan a peck.

"Good night," I said cheerily, and turned out the light.

Night after night, I denied all my unpleasant emotions. My body had found a good weapon to sabotage the whole thing:

You don't want the dirty, disgusting, shameful parts of yourself? Then you don't get your desire either.

* * *

As my libido started to shrivel under the spotlight of intimate attention, I found a solution that is predictable to people who've had affairs and baffling to those who haven't.

I started flirting again, with other women.

It felt sexy and even safer in some ways to imagine being desired by people who knew nothing about me.

Eve and I were sitting with another friend on the curb at one of Austin's food truck parks, munching on falafel sandwiches, when I realized I thought Eve was sexy. I liked how she wore her black hair in a ruler-straight cheek-length bob, like a French model. How her dense spattering of freckles concentrated your eyes just under hers. How, in her black muscle tank and high-waisted chinos, she somehow made everyone else look overdressed.

She was complaining to me and another friend about how hard dating was and how she wanted intimacy, but she was tired of dating, tired of taking the time to vet people and find someone new.

Before I could help myself, I blurted out, "Maybe you should make out with your friends."

And then I left to go to the bathroom. As I walked away, I found myself hoping she would think I meant me.

In the stall, Radio K started up. *You just don't know when to quit, do you? You already get nervous that Jordan and Christine will each want sex every time they see you, and now you're flirting with someone else. Tsk, tsk.*

Then that quiet, gentle voice piped up again: *It's okay to feel sexy. I know you don't see that yet, honey. You're looking outside yourself for what is already inside you.*

I looked hard in the mirror as I washed my hands. I didn't know how to stop looking outside myself—for love, for comfort, for validation of my worth. And because my relationships could never fill the hole inside myself, I reached outside of them too.

I mentally beat myself up and withheld love from myself—and it made me insatiable.

I brushed off that gentle voice, primped my hair, and applied lip balm. *Just relax and see what happens,* I compromised. *It's just flirting.*

Which was, frankly, a lie.

When I came back out of the bathroom, Eve was telling some story to our friend, gesturing with her hands. She stopped mid-sentence to look me up and down as I approached. I felt my skin break out in goosebumps, thrilled at her attention. I didn't hear any of the words she was saying. I just watched her move.

Eve was an actress—or more accurately, a drama teacher—and she knew exactly how mesmerizing her movements were. You could tell by how slowly she blinked, how she stood with her hips slightly forward but bent down with her back slightly arched. Her grace didn't look self-conscious to me; it looked self-assured. Eve said what was on her mind, and sometimes she was even sarcastic and bitchy. Somehow her bitchiness made her sexy.

Eve didn't yet know that I got anxious, that I shut down and went blank when my emotions got too intense, that I walled off when someone asked what I wanted. In flirting with Eve, I could start from scratch. Eve was wild. Around her, I could try to show off a wilder version of myself that didn't get so hung up on the tangled thoughts in my head.

Of course, true wildness is unbridled. But in trying to show just one side of myself, I was reining in all the rest. I was the opposite of wild. I didn't see that at the time because I was shoving all my emotions down. Much safer, I assumed, to *think* my way through all my problems than to deal with my feelings.

If I really wanted to be wild, I would have to feel everything. I was terrified of that. I thought for sure everyone would stop loving me, and then where the fuck would I be?

18

Time Share

Eve and I made plans to go see a documentary a few days later. We'd have dinner beforehand. No one chooses a documentary for a date movie, so it was easy to keep lying to myself.

I agonized way too long about getting dressed. *What says, "I like you and I feel sexy, but not really?"* We met up at a ramen shop. I had not thought about how messy ramen is to eat; I immediately second-guessed my white embroidered tank. Come to think of it, ramen was a terrible choice for the first time eating in front of someone. *Anyone—not just a date,* I told myself. Eve hugged me, and I couldn't stop staring at her lips, which were the same light pink as her sunglasses.

We ate, and the conversation was so easy that I got wrapped up in it and absentmindedly flicked droplets of red-orange broth all over my clothes. I tried not to care. But when we wrapped up dinner, I asked if we could stop by Deb's place so I could change. We were friends, I assured myself. *Friends don't care about embarrassing themselves in front of each other. Stop feeling so anxious about every little thing.*

I only closed the door halfway while I peeled the tank off and pulled another shirt on. I wondered if Eve peeked through the crack in the door.

But by the end of that night, I really wanted to see her again. And I didn't want to just see her—I wanted to kiss her. I kept Altoids in my purse that I would pop in my mouth and quickly crush in my teeth, hoping my breath didn't smell bad, even though I didn't expect we'd get close enough for her to notice whether it did or not.

Finally, one night Eve said, "I like you. I think I could *really* like you, if I let myself. Where is this relationship going for you? Casual or serious?"

I squirmed a little and bit the inside of my lip. "Do you plan out relationships like that? I tend to just let things unfold."

"I put more time and energy into people I'm serious about. When a relationship is casual, I pull myself back more so I don't get too involved." She made it sound so simple.

"I've never thought of relationships that way before," I said. "I try to show up however it feels right in the moment." This was partially true. I wasn't conscious of the ways it wasn't true—the ways I guarded myself and let my anxiety put walls between me and other people.

Choosing to get serious with Eve meant I had to acknowledge my inability to get truly intimate with Jordan or with Christine. I thought choosing to say no to her would mean shutting the door on the excitement and sexual energy I could feel coming back to my body.

Eve sat silently, waiting for me to say more.

"I like you," I said. "I have two partners already, and I'm constantly back and forth between Tucson and Austin. I'm not really sure how available I am with my time or my emotional capacity. I honestly don't know where this is going. I just know that I enjoy spending time with you, and I want to keep doing that."

"Okay," was all Eve said back.

I walked her out to her car to leave, and she stood there for what seemed like half a second too long before she opened her car door. In that tiny space of waiting, I leaned forward and kissed her. She made a little "mmm" sound that just about made me want to die.

Nice little trap you created, Radio K says. *Another person for you to not have sex with.*

But since I finally felt sexy again, I texted Eve. *Sweet dreams.*

* * *

Am I going to have a romantic relationship with this woman or not? The question scared me. Did I really want to schedule myself so tightly, with every night a date night with one of my partners, or a flight to go between them? Would the charge I felt for Eve help me access my sex drive with Jordan and Christine? Or would I sink into the same cycle all over again and push everyone away? Would I have time to spend with my friends? Time to spend with myself?

Did I even want to spend time with myself? My stomach tightened in a knot anytime I considered that. I knew if I spent time alone, I'd start feeling things.

But since I'd started meeting up with Eve, my libido had roared back. On my last date with Christine, we'd started out by playing an elaborate game of cards. Ten minutes in, I was losing. Christine was gloating.

"I don't want to play anymore," I pouted, only half-joking, and I threw down my fistful of cards. They scattered everywhere, some flipped face up, and I crawled through the mess on my knees to knock her cards out of her hand. Then I kissed her and wrapped my legs around her waist. We left the cards where they were and went to her bedroom.

I wanted sex with Jordan, too. We were on the couch in our Tucson house watching a show one night, and he looked over at me and smiled.

"Want me to go down on you?" he asked.

I hesitated for a second. We'd had sex with the TV on before, and I felt distracted, unable to relax with Leslie Knope shouting in excited indignation on *Parks and Recreation*. But I smiled and nodded and watched him while he pulled off my shorts. I lay back on the couch, still staring at him.

"Watch the show," he said. "Relax."

I giggled and turned my eyes back to the TV. The show was funny, and I laughed, and the pleasure from Jordan's touch made my laughter even bigger and more delightful. I lasted about two minutes before I wasn't paying attention to the show anymore and I wasn't distracted or annoyed by it either.

In those weeks of flirting with Eve, my anxiety let up, so long as I didn't try to think about the future and where all my relationships were headed.

I kept telling myself to stay in the moment and see how things evolved. Which really meant I didn't want to decide. Because then I'd have to get honest about what I wanted and why I wanted it.

I'd have to consider why I was always *looking* for what I wanted in someone new, instead of letting myself *receive* it from the people who loved me.

To let love in, I'd have to acknowledge I was worthy of it.

I want to go back in time and tell myself, *You need to think about what you want. Then you need to let people in before you do something stupid.*

* * *

I didn't tell Christine about Eve. Jordan knew I was going on dates with Eve, but I didn't tell him I hadn't talked to Christine about it. I told myself I didn't need to say anything because Christine and I had an open relationship anyway; we were allowed to date other people. I told myself Christine was stressed with work and troubles with her ex, and I didn't want to add to the chaos.

My hesitation to "add to the chaos" would have revealed two things if I'd been paying attention.

First: I thought myself to be the arbiter of Christine's stress.

Second: I knew bringing Eve into my life wasn't just about being sexy and playful. Dating a third person brought much more complexity into my life. I wasn't *choosing* more complexity, I told myself—it was just what happened when I refused to think about what I was doing.

Christine and I were going to meet up one afternoon while I was in Austin, and I told myself I was going to muster up the courage to tell her about Eve. When her car rolled up, I watched through the window. She took a few extra beats to turn off the engine. I saw her sigh. She got out of the car stiffly, shoulders pulled forward. I went down to the street and gave her a hug. Her arms were rigid at first. I held her tighter, and her shoulders relaxed just a little. The weight of her arms settled on my shoulders.

"What's wrong?" I asked, and Christine just shook her head. I ushered her inside, and she curled up with her legs crossed on the couch.

"Do you want some tea? I've got that ginger mint tea you love," I said. It was a hot day, but I knew tea was comforting to her. She nodded, and I made a cup for each of us. When I came back to the couch and settled in, Christine spilled out the latest saga with her ex-wife. Her ex's parents were ailing and lived in a different state, and after a recent stint in the hospital, the ex was thinking of relocating to care for them. Christine was trying to think through what was best for the kids.

"I think I might move," she said.

My heart stopped for a moment. *What would that mean for us?* I thought, but I knew it was too early to ask. What her boys needed was far more important. I willed my face not to show the grief flooding into my system. Right next to the grief was anger that she might so easily abandon me. I didn't want to show how I felt because I didn't want her to feel bad.

Christine talked through her options and how she felt about each one. She talked about her family and her ex and her kids. She didn't talk about us, though she ended with, "It's a beautiful place to visit."

I felt angry, and I was incredibly embarrassed at feeling angry. *How could I be angry when she's the one who might have to uproot her whole life? When I'm the one already living between cities?* I swallowed my anger and tried to help her feel excited about what opportunities might be in a new state.

It was easy to push my own feelings away. My news was inconsequential in comparison to hers. Her pain allowed me to play bedside nurse, to be the one in our relationship to hold the playfulness and the comfort. Her pain took the pressure off us having sex, and we spent a lot of time just holding each other.

I refused to spoil all the comforting by telling her I'd started dating someone else.

I was terrified, selfishly, of the fallout. I didn't want to break Christine's heart further. But it wasn't so much about me caring for her as it was about not wanting her to hate me.

If I told Christine, I'd have to let go of control over how she or anyone else might feel or react to my desires. I'd have to be willing to let my life change. I'd have to let people come in and out of my life. I'd have to let them love me and not love me, depending on what felt right to *them*. I wouldn't be able to control it.

• • •

On my next date with Eve, we were hanging out at her house when she pulled something up on her phone and then tossed her phone to me.

"Have you ever taken one of these quizzes?" she asked.

There on the screen were questions like, "Do you like to be tied up?" "If you're given a direct command by your master, do you like to talk back?" It was a kink quiz. For each question, I was meant to rate how interested I was from zero to five. I had never been asked questions like this before. For the first time I wondered what I would like and not like, what I might ask for and not ask for.

I filled out the quiz with a secret thrill in my stomach. *Fuck it,* I thought, *you might lose Christine anyway. Just let yourself do what feels good now.*

But then my stomach turned.

It was definitely time to tell Christine.

19

The Worst Lie
I Ever Told (Part 2)

The next night Christine and I got together, she was a mess over the situation with her ex, venting about their recent fight and the prospect of moving. It was the worst possible time to tell her. I gave her a long hug as she finished her story, and when we pulled away from each other, there was a pause.

This is when you have to say it, I thought, and my stomach flipped like I was jumping off a cliff. I spilled it all out at once.

"I started seeing someone. Her name is Eve. My relationship with you means so much to me, and it's because our relationship is so strong that—" I had to pause to swallow a lump in my throat. "That I feel like my capacity has grown and I'm ready to explore this new relationship with Eve."

Well, didn't you just dip this news in the sweetest sugar-coat you could find, Radio K sneered at me. I told myself that if I saw all of this in a positive light, maybe Christine would too, and maybe she wouldn't get hurt.

Christine's eyes got watery, but she didn't cry outright. She smiled. "That's nice." Then her brow furrowed a little. "How long have you been seeing her?"

How do I answer this question? From our first date, two months ago, or from the time I finally felt certain I wanted to see Eve for real? "A few weeks," I said vaguely.

Christine took a few measured breaths. "I would have wanted to know this sooner. I would have thought you would tell me when you were *interested* in someone. But you're not just interested; you're dating her."

"Yes," I said. "I'm really sorry. I just…I didn't know what I wanted, or what I wanted to do about it." I knew it sounded lame.

Christine shifted in her seat. "I would have thought you would have told me, not just as a girlfriend, but because friends share that kind of stuff with each other."

My cheeks burned and my breath suddenly got shallow. The bones of my sternum and ribs suddenly felt so heavy. I nodded. She was right: for months, I'd barely told Christine anything about myself. I usually just said work was fine, my flight was fine, Jordan was fine, everything was fine. "Fine" had lost so much meaning that it eventually became a lie.

"I was scared," I said. "I'm really sorry."

Christine nodded, and then she pulled me close and nestled her face into my neck. "It's okay," she said. "I just want to know a lot sooner next time."

I nodded. A hollow feeling settled somewhere at the bottom of my ribs. *Are you capable of doing better? Will you be able to open your mouth the next time you have to start an uncomfortable conversation?* I felt sick and ashamed.

Despite her kind words and her cuddling, I could feel extra tension in her shoulders. Her hands were rigid. Her breathing was shallow. So was mine. I couldn't relax into the couch. My legs started to feel restless. I didn't know where to put my hands. I started to feel really uneasy.

"Are you sure you're okay?" I asked, which wasn't really a question about her, but a question about me.

Christine answered honestly: she was angry. And sad. And concerned about health issues with another partner in my life. She was worried about my time and whether I'd still have enough for her.

I suddenly had the urge to pee, and I got up to go to the bathroom.

It turned out I didn't have to pee. I was just carrying that much tension in my body. I flushed the toilet anyway and washed my hands. I looked at myself in the mirror and tried to breathe, but I thought my reflection looked ugly and dumb.

As the weight of Christine's concerns started to sink in, I panicked.

Back on the couch, I blurted out, "I'm not sure it's going to work out with Eve. I think I might need to tell her I don't want us to date anymore."

The statement was out of my mouth before I realized the unconscious codependent tendency that drove it. I wanted to do anything in that moment to start fixing this mess I'd made. By which I mean, I wanted to do whatever I could to take away Christine's discomfort because I couldn't take it.

I knew it wasn't the right thing to say. I knew it wasn't actually going to fix anything. I knew it wasn't what I really wanted.

And I also knew—for the first time—that I was betraying myself.

*   *   *

I was confused enough by my conversation with Christine that I thought maybe I *did* want to stop seeing Eve. In the days after telling Christine I was dating Eve, I suddenly wanted to be alone all the time. Every night was filled with some plan to see someone—one night with Christine, the next with Eve, then with Christine again, then back home to Jordan—and I suddenly felt like I needed way more time to think. I needed time to come back to myself.

I realized with no small amount of dread that dating three people meant three people who could be upset or unhappy at three different times. I wanted to pull away from the whole world, to just read books and never talk to anyone again.

The next night I hung out with Eve, I thought I was going to tell her we should stop dating. *Did you catch that?* Radio K asked. *Framing it with a "we" like I can somehow make it a joint decision and avoid taking full responsibility?*

But we had a really nice time, and I realized *No, I just got myself all turned around.* We went for a walk along Walnut Creek during the golden hour, when the light filtered orange-pink through the trees.

"You asked before whether our relationship would be casual or serious," I finally said. "I'm still not sure what my emotional capacity is for this."

Saying a thing like that is like cracking the escape hatch on an airplane without jumping out. I didn't want to jump, but I wasn't sure how I'd be able to stay with all the wind rushing around.

I waited. Waited to see if Eve was going to jump out of the hatch first. If she did, it wouldn't have to be me who jumped.

"Well, now that I know you more, I'm kinda hooked." Eve nudged me with her shoulder. I felt guilty. *What side of myself have I been showing her? She needs to know I'm a monster.* But I felt comforted by her attention too. Since I didn't want to ruin the comfort, I didn't say anything more.

We walked until the sky went teal, then navy. Then we picked our way back along the creek, following its silver trail in the twilight.

* * *

When I finally went to see a therapist about all of this, months from this moment, she asked if I was in denial during this time. I told her no. The answer flew quickly out of my mouth. The therapist raised her eyebrows, just slightly, as though it were involuntary. She didn't ask any follow-up questions. Later, I thought, *Denial? What does that even mean?*

That's how little I was able to see what was going on in my own life at this moment.

I kept dating Eve, and I didn't tell Christine I'd backed out of breaking up with her. Christine never revisited the conversation, never asked whether I'd followed through, and after a few weeks I forgot about it.

Sometimes I forget important things like a friend's birthday or their parents' names, and when I'm talking to the friend in question my mind fritzes out because I'm trying to recall everything I've ever heard them say about themselves and their families. This was different; it was more like when I was with Christine, I erased all the important things about myself and tried to fill in the blanks with what she wanted me to be.

My memory held on to the fact that I'd told her I was dating Eve, not my half-hearted attempt to take it back, and for several weeks I thought there was nothing more to say about it.

My unconscious needed to protect me because I believed I was responsible for what Christine felt. When I saw Christine cry or shake in anger over some fight she'd had with her ex, I thought, *I don't ever want to make her feel like that.* I needed her to think of me as a good person. I hadn't fully formed my own sense of self-trust yet, and in its absence, I trusted her opinion of me.

If she thought I was bad, that meant I was. I would do anything to avoid making her cry.

• • •

While I was unspooling my codependent drama with Christine, the gear shop where Jordan still worked hit an economic downturn and furloughed most of the staff. Jordan was suddenly looking ahead to months without a job, and he debated whether he even wanted to go back. He decided to come to Austin with me. I got a short-term apartment for the two of us, and we drove out together.

The first time Jordan and Christine met, they were cordial and stiff with each other. Meanwhile I felt like a grade-schooler trying to get two new friends to bond. I wanted my loved ones to want to spend time together so that I wouldn't feel like I was living a double life. They seemed disinterested.

But when Jordan and I went to a birthday party for a friend of Eve's, Jordan pointed Eve out and said he thought she was attractive. At some point later that night, when I was feeling wild and impulsive and sexy, I whispered in Eve's ear, "You know, Jordan is into you, too."

As the party wound down, Jordan and I said our goodbyes and headed out the front door, and just after we closed it, the front door opened and closed again.

Eve was standing close to the two of us. "Let's all go home."

"Whose home?" Jordan asked.

"Yours." Eve said.

I could feel my eyes widening. "You mean, sleep together?"

She nodded, smiling.

I looked at Jordan, who nodded. I nodded fervently to both of them. "Meet you at our place."

My brain loves threesomes. So often during sex, I'm thinking all the time—about how I look, where I should look, how I smell, whether my touch is gentle enough or rough enough, whether I'll get enough sleep when it's over.

And sure enough, when Jordan and Eve started undressing each other, I stood back a little, vibrating with energy and totally unsure what to do. Eve grabbed my shirt and pulled me to her, and then we were kissing, and her hands were on me, and Jordan's hands were on me, and my brain finally shut the fuck up and gave up on trying to manage it all.

My body took the reins. For a few blissful, thoughtless hours, I took the lead when I wanted to, and I surrendered when I wanted to. No agonizing necessary. I had orgasms just from listening to orgasms.

. . .

Christine's ex decided not to move in the end. They'd made arrangements for the ailing parents, and the long-term picture looked promising, at least for now. Christine told me this while we were sitting on the couch, and her eyes looked bright again. Things were resolving with her ex, and she was feeling more settled. When she finished her update, she sighed, and her face relaxed. I told her about the threesome.

As she listened, her eyes got glassy with tears. "I knew you and Jordan were looking for a third," she said. "So I guess that makes sense. I just didn't realize you were still interested in Eve."

I nodded. The tears never fully fell down from Christine's eyelids; they just sat on the rims of her eyes, quivering. She tucked her head under my chin, her cheek resting against my collarbone. I hugged her. I felt a wet spot spread on my shirt.

I could feel my anxiety creeping in. I suddenly got the urge to fidget and get up from the couch, but I didn't move because Christine was resting against me. *Don't get upset that she's upset*, I thought. *Don't take the truth back just because it makes her uncomfortable. It's still the truth.*

I felt Christine take a deeper breath, and then she lifted her head. "I love you," she said.

It was the first time either of us had said it to the other. I felt an explosion of happiness spread through my chest.

"I love you too. I've been wanting to say that for a while now." I hugged her tight and kissed the side of her neck. Tears of relief started to well up. *Maybe I didn't break us after all.*

"I realized I wanted to say it back when you thought you were going to move. I was devastated by that because I love you. But I didn't want to say it because I knew that decision was hard and confusing already." I paused. "I love you," I said again, and Christine kissed me for a long time. It was one of the last kisses between us that felt real.

20

How a Secret
Becomes a Bomb

The next weekend, Christine and I were taking an overnight trip together to San Antonio. She had a work gig she needed to travel for, and we decided to take the opportunity to spend the night together.

She showed up at the door in the morning, and I could tell something was off. Her hand movements were jerky. Her whole body was shaking almost imperceptibly.

"Are you okay?" I asked.

"Yes," she said as she busied herself shoving bags into my van. Her voice was flat. She didn't look up. Her *yes* seemed like a *no*. I assumed it had something to do with her ex again.

Denial is an incredibly powerful, numbing drug. It wasn't until we were trapped in traffic on I-35 that I realized I'd broken her heart.

"You were dating her the whole time, weren't you?" Her voice sounded rough, like she'd been crying already.

I opened my mouth to answer, and then I froze. I stared straight forward out the windshield with my mouth open for a second. I finally closed it and nodded. My hands quivered on the steering wheel.

Christine said nothing. I looked at her out the corner of my eye. She was staring out the windshield too, eyes wide. I could see a vein popping in her temple.

"What are you feeling?" I asked quietly.

"I'm furious," she said quickly. She didn't elaborate.

We'd entered high-speed traffic, and my eyes bounced from the side-view mirrors to the rearview. I looked over my shoulder to check my blind spot three times before changing lanes. I thought for sure one of the cars would come up from behind and hit us.

"It's like you're this giant stomping around," Christine said finally. Her voice was thin and reedy. "You're walking around crushing all these trees and houses and people and you don't realize it. You just go on your merry way, and never look down to see who you're squashing." She quickly wiped tears from the sides of her eyes and turned her face away to the side window.

"I'm so sorry," I said.

Christine didn't turn her head to look back. My mouth was watering with the kind of sour saliva that comes up right before I throw up. I wondered if I could roll down the window and manage to vomit on the outside of the door without getting any inside. The traffic was too choked to pull over. "I'm really sorry," I said again.

"You hid the fact that you were dating her the first time. For weeks. And I told you—I *told you* I wanted you to communicate better if it happened again."

I nodded. "I'm so sorry. I forgot that I'd told you I might break up with her, and I didn't revisit that conversation with you." *How did I fucking forget that?* I screamed silently to myself.

I white-knuckled the steering wheel as my worst thoughts cycled through my brain. *You're so stupid and inconsiderate. You don't care about anyone but yourself.*

I was sure Christine was thinking the same things about me. She shook her head and bit her thumbnail as she stared out her window.

I took measured breaths, trying to calm myself down despite feeling completely trapped in the hot car.

"What would help right now?" I asked.

"I don't know," Christine shrugged. "Nothing. I just need time."

I turned the air conditioner to full blast, trying to stave off some of the heat beating through the windshield. I tried to think of what music we could put on that might soothe her a little. *What music does she like?* I couldn't remember. The only artist that came to me was Billie Eilish, but there was no way I was putting on her dark, haunting melodies. *I can't even remember what kind of music my girlfriend likes,* I thought. *Do I really not pay enough attention to remember something so simple?*

Years later, I still remember a lot of Christine's favorite music. I understand myself well enough now to know I draw a blank when I'm overwhelmed. I didn't know myself that well at the time, so I beat myself up for everything I couldn't remember.

*   *   *

Christine had cooled down a bit by the time we got to our house rental. We lugged in our bags and set them by the front door. The place was small, a studio space with a loft bed opposite the kitchen. Under the loft was a little den with a couch and crappy lamps with scarves draped over them to create a cheap bohemian effect. Dotted around the house were little statuettes and meditation beads. A desk in the corner had little affirmation notes scattered all around. *I love my body and honor its wisdom.*

Someone is working hard to love themselves, Radio K snarked.

"It's cute!" Christine said, and I couldn't tell if her cheerfulness was genuine or not. "I feel like a martini," she added. "Let's find a liquor store."

We walked the neighborhood until we stumbled on a little market. We bought wilted salads for dinner, a bottle of gin, and a quart-sized jar of olives because they didn't have anything smaller.

We split the bill, and a flush of embarrassment rolled through me when I saw how much we were paying to numb ourselves. I said nothing. The gin seemed like an absolute necessity.

Back at the house, we made martinis and things seemed to soften a little. I tried to make her laugh. I drank two martinis and quickly started to feel cloudy. The salad had been mostly lettuce. I stopped drinking. Christine fixed more cocktails, eyeballing the measurements.

Sometime around midnight, she downed what was left in her glass and turned to look me square in the face. "I was really upset earlier," she said, "but I'm feeling better now."

Then she pulled me in close, kissed me, and grabbed the back of my hair harder than I like.

"It's going to be okay," she hissed in my ear. "I love you. I'm just really fucking mad at you." She growled—what sounded to me like a guttural, screeching yowl—and she grabbed my shoulders, digging in her nails just a little, and shook me. I was pretty sure she was trying to be playful, but her actions scared me. There seemed to be a little too much edge to them. She let me go and went to pee.

I glanced over at the bottle of gin on the counter. There was much more missing than made sense to me.

I thought about leaving. Maybe I could still find a hotel in the middle of the night, or I could drive to a different neighborhood and sleep in the back of my car. I could pick her up at the end of the trip and drive her back home.

But the thought of leaving had barely formed before it flew out of my mind again. Christine hadn't come back from the bathroom. Behind the curtain that hung in place of a door, I saw her curled on the bathroom floor. I heard her sob.

"Are you okay?" I asked. I walked over and crouched next to her. She clutched the edges of the toilet. She didn't look like she was going to throw up. It seemed more like she was trying to steady herself.

"I got drunk on purpose," she said. She looked at me, and her cheeks were streaked with tears. "I wanted to lose some inhibition so I could let myself feel this. I need to feel it so I can let it go."

Then Christine seemed to heave with sobs. I nodded and wrapped my arms around her. "It's okay. I understand," I said, though I wasn't sure I did. She took in shaky breaths, and I could tell her nose was plugged up. I reached up overhead and unrolled a big wad of toilet paper. She took it and blew her nose. She seemed to calm for a moment, and then another wave of grief came over her.

I wrapped my arms around her again, but this time she shoved my arms away. I crouched awkwardly, inches away from her. I had no idea what to do.

"Hold me," she said in a strained voice.

"I'm sorry," I said, "you just pushed me—"

She grabbed my arm and pulled me toward her. "I need you to hold me even when I push back. I need to know you'll stay here with me even if I push you away."

I was so confused, but I did as I was told. She cried until she slumped down on the floor, exhausted.

"Let's get you to bed," I said. "You'll be more comfortable there."

Christine didn't answer me. I brought her a glass of water, which she gulped down. I brought a blanket over and wrapped her up, tucking her in between the toilet and the sink. We stayed like that for what seemed like hours, not speaking. I held Christine as each new wave came through, and in the brief moments of calm I readjusted myself to try to ease the cramping in my back.

My emotions came in waves too. Sometimes I felt capable of staying by her side and holding her. I felt strong. Then my throat would close up and I just wanted to run away. I thought about getting up to walk around the block or crawling into bed and putting in earplugs. Anything to try to change the situation. I stayed crouched by Christine until I felt strong again, and then I held her tighter.

I finally got her to crawl over to the bed around four or five in the morning. I set an alarm for eight, when Christine needed to get up to get ready for work.

Look at all the harm I've done, I lay in bed thinking. *I will never be able to forgive myself.*

I know now that forgiveness is a kissing cousin of acceptance. I didn't understand that at the time. I hung on to my sense of wrong-doing because I couldn't accept the parts of myself I'd hidden from Christine. The part of me that wanted to be sexual and intimate with her but couldn't bring myself to be vulnerable. The part of me that was willing to break her trust to hide myself. The part of me that was scared of the push-pull of love between us and added another partner to my life to diffuse it.

I needed Christine to forgive me. Maybe if she did, I could bypass the seemingly insurmountable task of forgiving myself for what I'd done to her.

Christine roused just in time to throw on fresh clothes, wet her hands, and smooth away the bed head before going to her morning staff meeting. I hugged her, and she held me for a long time. She felt so warm that I let myself relax for a moment. I tried to focus on the smell of her apricot lotion.

"Do I feel like I've got a fever?" she asked as she pulled away. Christine lifted my palm to her forehead. I brought my other hand to my own forehead, comparing us. We felt the same.

"If you do, I do too," I said. "I think we're okay."

She gave me a weak smile. "Let's find coffee on the way."

* * *

When I picked Christine up after her seminar, she seemed energized. She talked about how well her presentation went and the great feedback she'd gotten. I'd spent the day at the coffee shop, trying to work but mostly thinking about what an awful person I was.

As we drove back to Austin, Christine put a song on the radio. I heard the opening beats of "Fallingwater" by Maggie Rogers.

"Will you sing?" Christine asked.

"Fallingwater" is a belting anthem kind of song. The kind that takes your whole body to sing. My throat felt dry. I kept my hands glued to ten and two and checked the rearview mirror instead of looking her in the eye.

"I don't know—"

"I really want to hear you sing," Christine said.

I felt heartbroken. I thought back to when I was young, and how when my mom was upset, I would put on her favorite Phoebe Snow albums. My mom always sang along, and if she didn't join in, I knew something was really wrong. I wondered if Christine was trying to use the same kind of gauge on me. I really didn't feel like singing. Christine started humming.

I tried to hit the first note quietly, but my voice felt choked. I took a deeper breath and let the next line come out as loud as it needed to. I let my throat relax. The corners of my eyes filled with tears, and I forced myself not to blink so they wouldn't fall down my cheeks. I was belting now, and Christine touched my arm gently. I pried my hand off the steering wheel to lace my fingers in hers.

For one song, I breathed a little easier. I wanted this easiness to stay, but when the next track turned on, I was jolted out of the moment. Radio K started listing off all the reasons I should be hating myself instead of singing.

21

Up in Smoke

The week after Christine and I got back, I met up with Eve at her apartment. I felt nervous as I knocked on her door. I was going to tell her we needed to stop dating. I knew I wanted to phrase it that way—somehow it seemed more fitting than "we need to break up." *Breakups are for girlfriends,* I thought, and we weren't quite that. We were something more casual than a full-blown relationship but more serious than casual sex.

I took a breath. *It's going to be fine,* I thought. *Just be honest with where you're at.*

But don't be too honest, Radio K interjected. *You're a mess, and you don't want to show her all that.*

In the few days since we'd been back, I'd compulsively checked my phone every two minutes or so, looking for texts from Christine.

I was on high alert, constantly wondering, *How is Christine doing? Is she feeling better about us yet? Does she need anything from me?*

I knew I'd broken her trust, and I wanted to show her I was trustworthy. In my mind, that meant responding to her the instant she reached out for me.

I needed to end things with Eve not because there was something wrong between her and me, but because things felt so wrong with Christine—and I felt wholly responsible to fix them—that I had no energy for anyone else. Not even Jordan. I'd devolved into a sullen roommate who talked very little and watched a lot of TV.

Eve opened the door and greeted me with a new bottle of mezcal in her hands and asked if I wanted a cocktail. Her excitement threw me off guard and cut through my somber mood for a moment. I smiled and said "sure," and she opened the door wider and gestured for me to sit on the couch.

I tried to lean back and relax as Eve busied herself making mezcal sours at the kitchen counter. She poured the drinks into two hand-blown rocks glasses and winked at me as she sat down.

I took a slow sip, savoring the sharp tang and the lingering smoke. I wanted to drink the whole thing ever so slowly before I began talking, but I knew I couldn't put off what I had come here to say.

I lowered my drink and looked down into the glass. "So, there's something I need to talk to you about. I have not done a good job in talking to Christine about my relationship with you. I didn't communicate with her while I was trying to get clear about what I wanted my relationship with you to look like. I didn't tell her when we started dating initially—I only told her a few weeks ago."

I took another sip and thought about how to phrase the next part. I left out the part about telling Christine I thought I needed to end things with Eve. "She's having a hard time with my lack of communication around that—understandably so—and I need to take a step back and focus on repairing things with her. I need to stop dating you."

When I looked up at Eve's face, she was looking back at me. Her face was neutral. She didn't say anything.

"I'm still interested in getting closer to you, as a friend," I said, averting my eyes to the window. "And I may even have more capacity in the future to bring the sexual and romantic components back. But right now, I need to take a step back."

Eve's ferret started playing with a string on the floor, and I turned my head to watch him tumble. He got the string tangled around one paw and tried in vain to shake it off.

When I looked back up, Eve was wiping tears from her face.

"Are you okay?" I asked.

"Yes," she said. "I understand. It just sucks. I really like you, and I liked where this was going. I don't know if I can just be friends."

I nodded. I felt guilty. I knew I'd unconsciously constructed this whole setup because I'd been in denial about how I felt. That small, soft voice had been whispering lately, *You need time to learn how to be honest—first with yourself, and then with everyone else.*

It was important to me to heal my relationship with Christine because it was the only way I could think of to prove to myself that I could be better. I didn't know then how to trust growth just within myself. I thought the only way to heal was to see my healing reflected in someone else. *I'll only know I've been forgiven if Christine forgives me.*

It never occurred to me that I could heal and come into deeper integrity with myself, and other people still might not feel ready or able to trust me or love me. Because I couldn't separate myself from my relationships, I used the love of others as my metric for how much to love myself.

"How long do you think this will be?" Eve asked.

I looked up from my almost-empty glass. "What?"

"You said you might be able to have a romantic or sexual relationship in the future. How long do you think that might be?"

I shook my head. "I have no idea. I'm realizing I need to do some deep-level work on myself. I have a hard time being clear and up-front with what I'm feeling."

"Not in my experience," Eve said.

I teared up. I wanted that to be true. But since I knew I hadn't shared openly with her either, it didn't feel true at all. I didn't say anything. I just downed the rest of my cocktail and set the glass down.

"Thank you," I said. "And I'm sorry for hiding my relationship with you from Christine."

Eve stood up, and we hugged. She held on a long time. I broke away first and said goodbye as I let myself out.

22

Push and Pull

A text from Christine lit up my phone. She wanted to know if I could come by her office. She needed to tell me something. My guts churned.

Her text came through a few days after we got back, in the middle of a workday. It pinged to my computer while I was editing a manuscript, and my stomach dropped.

She's going to break up with me, I thought.

I closed my laptop and looked out the window, not really taking in the waving branches on the tree outside. The sky was steel gray, immovable. I had a full afternoon of work ahead of me, but I knew I wouldn't be able to focus on any of it until I knew what she was going to say. I wanted to go to her. I was terrified to go.

I'm on my way, I texted back.

Rain started to splatter haphazardly on my car as I drove to her office. I focused on the mechanical swipes of the wipers, focused on staying between the lines on the road.

When I walked into Christine's office, she was smiling—a genuinely warm, calm, affectionate smile—and she pulled me in for a hug. I pressed my cheek into her chest and felt grateful she couldn't see my face, which was starting to contort around the tears I was trying not to let out. When we both pulled back from the hug, I saw I'd left a wet spot on her shoulder. I hoped she couldn't feel it.

"I just got off call with Tom," Christine said. Her best friend. "I called him for a little extra support this week. I feel a lot better, and I asked you over because I need to tell you—"

I broke down crying, wailing actually, and Christine couldn't finish her sentence. She caught me by the elbows as I hunched over, sobbing, and she gently lowered me to sit on the hardwood floor. I traced the weathered grain with my eyes while trying to slow down my breath. I didn't look at Christine's face until she crouched down further to meet my eyes.

"I'm not going to break up with you," she said. "Is that why you're crying?"

I nodded and made myself keep looking at her face even though I wanted to curl into a ball. There was a big dark knot in one plank of the wood, like a well or a wormhole, and I imagined being able to drop through the floor to some other place in the universe where I didn't feel so awful.

Christine smiled again, that same warm smile, and said, "I feel good. I wanted you to come over so I can tell you—I know we can make it."

Snot streamed down my upper lip, and I wiped it away with my sleeve just before Christine handed me a box of tissues. I felt a flash of anger—*Why couldn't you have texted that before I rushed here?*—but I brushed it away. It wasn't the "right" thing to feel when Christine seemed on the verge of forgiving me.

"How do you know?"

Christine shrugged. "I talked through the whole situation with Tom, and I also told him all the things I love about you, and he just said, 'Well, you got dinged up.' That feels right. I know we can work with a few dings. You're worth it."

I sobbed harder and tried to mop it all up with tissues, but they just became a soggy wad. I wanted to believe her, so I didn't say anything back. I wanted to let her words sink in, but they kept skating off.

There it was: Christine could accept me despite the dings I'd given her.

I know now that her acceptance wasn't what I was really seeking. At my core, I wanted to accept myself, and I couldn't. Christine was a proxy. Despite what she said, my inner narrative was still the same.

What kind of monster hurts someone like that?

* * *

The next week, Christine was supposed to come over for a date. I was on my period and felt sick with nausea, a migraine, and cramps that radiated down my thighs. I wanted to down painkillers and sleep, but I didn't think I could cancel on her. I still needed to prove to her that when I said I would do something, I would follow through.

So I wore leggings and a long-sleeved striped dress because they were the only comfortable things I could think of, even though the elastic of the leggings still dug right under my belly button, where the cramps felt the worst.

We sat on the floor and played a card game while I hugged a pillow to my belly. I kept shifting around, trying to get comfortable with my ass on the cement floor and my back against the bottom edge of the couch. I focused on the cards in my hands.

Christine won. I pretended to be pissed just so she could keep gloating. The competition was the only thing that kept us talking.

After the game, Christine gathered up the cards and I thought I caught a sigh.

"Want to pull tarot cards?" I asked, desperate for some middle ground between not talking and talking too much.

I didn't really understand tarot, but I'd just bought a deck of cards because the artwork was beautiful—pen-and-ink drawings of priestesses and animals, with watercolors splashing across them. I was desperate for these old archetypical images to tell me something about myself I couldn't see. Never mind that all the stories I constructed about them in my head were self-reinforcing anyway.

Christine looked at a few of the images and then shuffled the deck. "What question do you want to hold in mind?" she asked.

Suddenly I realized the hole in my plan: this was going to make me vulnerable. But I also knew the reason I was struggling with small talk and light moments was because there was still so much big, negative-seeming energy between us. So I leaned in.

"I want to know what the journey into healing our relationship is going to look like," I said.

Christine didn't say anything; she just took a deep breath and held the cards in her hands for a moment. Then she spread them all in a line face down, and we took turns pulling them.

The images on the cards looked happy, even joyful. The three of cups showed a trio of animals at a tea party. The page of cups held a decorated goblet and stroked the head of a hare at her side. The sun had a cow's skull surrounded by bright sunflowers and ripe fruit.

"This doesn't feel like it fits," Christine said.

"Really?" My voice pitched a few notes higher than usual.

"Let's pull one more," she said. "I often pull one overview card to set the tone of the spread."

Christine plucked one last card from the deck and turned it over. The five of wands. Two dogs fighting, mouths open to grapple with their teeth. A bird flew over the fray, squawking down at them as if begging them to stop.

Why did it have to be that one? I thought.

"That feels right to me," Christine said. Fuck the sun. We were dogs fighting to the bitter end.

At least if they're fighting, they're still in contact, I thought. And then I felt really, really tired and a cramp seared through my belly.

"I need to go to bed," I said.

"Okay." Christine gave me a long hug. "It's going to take time," she whispered in my ear, "but we can get through it."

I wiped away tears. "It's just my period," I said.

Why was I uncomfortable with Christine wanting to comfort me?

Because you're a cheater and a liar, Radio K answered, *and now your body is drumming up pain so you can get sympathy. You don't deserve it.*

That soft, tender voice in me came back, so quiet I barely caught what she said. *Your body is bringing up pain to ask you to stop and care for yourself. You deserve to love yourself.*

I started to cry. My blood pounded harder in my ears, and all my face muscles clenching just made my head hurt more.

I tried to explain to Christine what was going through my pain-drenched brain. "It's like I've opened Pandora's box, and it's all flooding in—all the shame and guilt and anger and desire —and it's all in this muddy, mixed-up mess. All these emotions are coming through at once and they've short-circuited my brain. I can't take it all at once, and I can't figure out how to feel them. I just want to stuff them back in the box, but I also know I can't."

Christine looked me straight in the eyes, and a bright warmth spread across her face that I couldn't understand. I had to look away because my own eyes couldn't focus.

"That's the thing," she said gently. "Once you see, you can't unsee."

I closed my eyes and blew my exhale out from pursed lips. "I can't handle looking at anything right now."

Christine put a warm hand on my arm. I kept my eyes closed and just tried to feel the weight of her hand.

"I know this part is really uncomfortable. This is how it begins," Christine said.

"How what begins?"

"Healing yourself."

Christine pulled me into a tight hug, my nose smashed against her collarbone. Her arms and the panic squeezed my ribs, and I couldn't take a deep breath, so I cried, and I felt ashamed.

"I'd like us to go to counseling together," Christine said. "I should have suggested that before. We've gone too long trying to figure this out on our own. It will be easier with help."

I think she felt me stiffen because she tightened her arms around me.

You can't go to counseling together, Radio K said. *It's not like you're married or have kids together. Couples counseling costs a bazillion dollars, and it's a lousy investment. You've fucked this up too badly to fix it.*

I want to fix it, though, I thought. *I love her.*

Some way you have of showing it, Radio K replied.

I wanted to say, "I love you," but I stopped myself. It was a desperate moment. I wanted to tell her I loved her when I really felt that love, not when I was panicked about losing love.

So instead, I just said, "Okay."

The next day I got another migraine.

23

Stone Walls

I liked our therapist's office. It had big cushy chairs on wheels so you could push them wherever you wanted them in the room. She had lamps around the room instead of overhead lights. A little white scent infuser sat in the corner giving off hints of lavender and rosemary. Rows of bookshelves filled the wall behind the therapist's chair, and the therapist kicked off her shoes and sat cross-legged in her overstuffed armchair. She took her time arranging a shawl around her shoulders and setting a large notebook to the side.

I sat down on one armchair, both my feet on the floor, my hands in my lap. I leaned back, but the chair was built for someone much bigger, so I had to scoot back to be fully supported. My feet dangled like a little kid's.

Christine piled her purse and coat in a spare chair against the wall and pushed the other big-wheeled armchair up to mine until the armrests were touching. Then she took off her shoes, curled up in the chair, and took my hand. Clearly everyone else in the room was far more comfortable than I was.

"So what brings you here today?" the therapist asked, adjusting her glasses and picking up a pen.

I looked over at Christine.

"We're looking for some tools to communicate better," Christine said, her voice calm and measured. "We've had a hard time connecting lately, and we've fallen into a bit of a pattern." Christine glanced at me and then turned back to the therapist. I just looked at Christine. "I've been feeling lots of strong emotions, and when I express them to Emily..."

"I have a hard time being there for her without getting really emotional myself," I broke in. It felt too weird for Christine to speak for me. The therapist nodded slowly.

"And then sometimes she withdraws," Christine added. The therapist nodded again.

"Has this always been the dynamic between the two of you?"

I shook my head and looked over at Christine. She was shaking her head too.

I took a deep breath and told the therapist about how I'd started seeing Eve and hadn't told Christine, and when I did, she was understandably upset. "And now when we talk about it, Christine experiences big emotions. I try to put my own emotions away so I can be there for her, but I get overwhelmed. I don't feel like I deserve to be upset because it's my fault, but I get overwhelmed anyway. We end up getting stuck in conversations because I can't control my emotions."

The therapist wrote something down in the notebook. "So it seems you vacillate between putting up walls and having no boundaries?"

I nodded. "I think that's right." I pulled my hand away from Christine's so I could adjust my seat in the too-big chair. I didn't put my hand back.

"What do you feel before you find yourself putting up a wall?" the therapist asked.

Blank. I felt it happening, felt the blank brain fog seep into my head. I felt embarrassed. *This can't happen here*, I thought. *This is where I came to fix it. I'll never fix it if I can't talk about it.*

I sat staring at the therapist for a moment until she reached to the side of her big chair and pulled a chart out from against the wall. The chart was oversized so she could hold it from across the room and her clients could read it. It had eight emotions listed down one column: anger, fear, pain, joy, passion, love, shame, guilt.

A second column listed out more emotions that were facets of the basic emotions. My eyes gravitated toward "embarrassed" next to shame. Then I found "apprehensive" and "overwhelmed" next to fear. "Lonely" sat next to pain.

A third column was labeled "their gifts," but my eyes mostly skipped over this column because I didn't understand it. *How do you get "humility, containment, and humanity" from shame? How do you get "energy" from anger? How do you get "wisdom and protection" from fear?*

My eyes skipped to the last column, which listed the places the eight emotions could be felt in the body, and the quality of the feeling. I gravitated toward the description under fear: *stomach, upper chest—suffocation.* I felt everything listed under shame: *face, neck, and/or upper chest—warm, hot, red.* And there was the *gut—gnawing sensation* of guilt that never seemed to let up.

"I think I feel fear, shame, and guilt mostly," I said. "And pain," I said as my eyes caught that column: *lower chest and heart—hurting.*

The therapist nodded and looked down at the chart. "This comes from a book you may find helpful to read. It's called *Facing Codependence.*"

"Codependence?" I asked.

"I'm not saying yet that's what you're experiencing," the therapist continued. "You may find aspects from the book that resonate with you, and you may not. We can explore that in a future session if you like."

I folded my hands in my lap and started to pick at a hangnail the others couldn't see. "I'm realizing I don't really know what codependency means in this context," I said.

"At a basic level, codependency can express as a tendency to feel you're not okay if Christine isn't okay."

My heart was pounding. That was exactly how I felt, so I was relieved she'd said it, but I was embarrassed to admit it felt true.

I nodded and tried not to blink too much so the tears wouldn't roll off my eyelids. I worried if I started crying now, we wouldn't get anything done in this hour and a half we had with the very expensive therapist.

"I'd like to try an experiment," the therapist said. Christine nodded, her face relaxed. I nodded, feeling nervous. "Sometimes it can be helpful just to get more sensitive to the degree of distance you need in any given moment. I'd like you to turn your chairs to face each other."

Christine and I got up and pulled our chairs apart from each other, twisting them into place a few feet away.

"Now Emily, back your chair up all the way to the wall and have a seat. Christine, I want you to move your chair to the distance that feels most comfortable for you."

I sat in my chair and watched as Christine pushed hers up close, less than two feet away. Our knees grazed each other. She gave me one of her charming bright-faced smiles. Christine used to smile like that a lot, just randomly, and sometimes after the smile she would blurt out, "You're amazing!" I never knew how to accept this, so I'd often just smile and parrot the line back to her. But it always made me feel good.

Remembering that, I giggled, and Christine giggled too.

After a few moments, the therapist asked us to switch chairs. Christine sat against the wall, and I sat down in her chair.

"Let's take a moment to reset," the therapist said. "Get up and push the chair all the way back to the other wall. Then adjust the chair to the distance that feels most comfortable."

I backed my chair all the way up, but it was too far, so I stood up a little and shuffled my feet forward as I pulled the bottom of the chair. I stopped six feet away and sat back down, then scooted my chair forward to three feet and sat for a while longer. My legs felt restless, and I wanted to pick at my hangnail again. So I pushed the chair back six inches, then six inches more.

By the time I stopped adjusting, I was five feet from Christine. We weren't giggling this time. Christine's face was impassive.

"Christine, how does this distance feel to you?" the therapist asked.

"It feels far," she said. Her voice was so small and quiet.

I tried to give her an encouraging smile, but I was actually feeling sad, and my lips tightened more than I meant them to. I wanted to want to be closer.

I thought about faking it and readjusting my chair again to pull it closer, but I didn't. I felt really agitated, caught between wanting to make Christine feel better and wanting to make myself feel better, because those days, they didn't ever seem to be the same thing.

• • •

We went to a few more sessions with the very expensive therapist. In one session, Christine was explaining to the therapist how she'd felt when I betrayed her, and she started to cry. I wanted to hug her, but we were in the big armchairs again that held each of us in a cushy box, and the half-wall arms were stacked between us.

"Emily, why don't you try comforting Christine in this moment? The physical space is awkward, but what if you try anyway and get a sense of navigating that?"

I nodded and reached over the tops of the bulky armrests to hug Christine around the shoulders, but I instantly saw how I was pulling her uncomfortably against the armrest. So I climbed on top of the armrests and leaned toward her to hold her head against my chest. My back started to ache as I leaned from one hip, but I ignored it.

Christine started to sob harder, and she wrapped her arms around my waist and pulled me in closer. I scooted toward her until I was off the armrest and in her lap, squeezed with her into the chair. It felt good to wrap my arms around her and hold her shaking body while she cried.

I tried to ignore the fact that I'd wound up in her lap like a small child.

Christine started to calm down, and her grip on me relaxed. I clambered off her, went back to my own seat, and held her hand, which was wrapped around a soggy tissue.

"It's really important to me to know that if you strike up another relationship with someone, or have some kind of slip up, we can talk about it," Christine said.

The therapist turned to me. "Do you think you can commit to being able to talk about any new relationships that develop?"

I could feel an internal wall going up. My rib cage felt wooden. "I definitely want to be able to," I said. "But I wanted to be able to talk about my mistakes back when I messed up then, too. I still don't understand why I couldn't. So I'm working on it. For now, I'm mostly focused on not making any mistakes."

The therapist raised her eyebrows almost imperceptibly. Christine's brow furrowed a little. I was trying so hard to answer honestly, and from their faces I could tell it wasn't the right answer.

"It's not about making mistakes or not," Christine said. "It's about being able to talk about what you think and feel."

I nodded. I dug my fingernail into the seam of my jeans. The pain helped me pull my attention away from my thoughts. I watched a tiny moth bat at the lampshade behind the therapist's head.

"I want to," I said.

• • •

A month or so into therapy, I had a dream that Christine was driving on an expressway, and I was in the front seat, navigating with a map that kept changing and redrawing itself. I was so confused; I'd tell Christine to take an exit only to realize at the last minute that the road was going to take us somewhere we didn't want to go, and I'd tell her not to take the exit and she would jerk the wheel to bring us back on the expressway.

We missed exit after exit, and after a while of trying to interpret the map, I realized the highway made a figure eight. We were driving along an infinity sign, a Möbius strip, and we had to get off somewhere, anywhere. I tossed the map away and pointed to the next exit that looked like it might be friendly. Christine took it, and I didn't redirect this time.

The road went up a steep hill lined with purple jacaranda trees, and it dead-ended in front of a stone wall.

Stone wall, Radio K snickered, *get it?*

The wall was covered in all these lush tropical vines. A riot of green. Beyond the wall was a house, and I had the sense that if we could just get to the house, we could live there, and everything would be okay.

I woke up before we got out of the car. My first thought was, *Thank god we at least got off the highway.*

I want to go back and tell this scared, confused version of me, *There are no mistakes. There are only circumstances, patterns, and choices. You're stuck in a loop of vilifying yourself, but when you're ready to step out of it—when you're ready to understand and hold compassion for the choices you've made—that's when you will truly grow.*

* * *

I felt so much shame in those months that it didn't feel like an emotion so much as just a fact of me. I was made of shame. The shame of wanting attention. Shame of wanting sex; shame of shying away from sex. The shame of keeping Eve a secret, and the shame of lying, which I realized were two different kinds of shame. The shame of being a shitty friend and a shaky partner.

As these patterns unfolded with Christine and consumed all my emotional energy and attention, I felt ashamed that I'd essentially suspended my relationship with Jordan. At home—*was our efficiency Austin apartment even a home?*—I became a zombie in front of the TV. We went on hikes in the Barton Creek Greenbelt, and I didn't want to talk. When I did talk, it was about Christine. I felt the shame of being self-absorbed, and I felt lonely. No one could touch me in this dark, tiny space shame had locked me in.

I felt grief too. The relationships I'd had were dead. I wasn't present with Jordan, I wasn't dating Eve, and things would never be the same with Christine. My relationship with myself had shattered. I didn't want to be with myself.

And I felt really fucking rageful. At random moments, the urge to cry would crash over me all at once. In the middle of one afternoon when I had the apartment to myself, I lay fully clothed on the middle of the bed and clutched the bedspread as tears welled in the corners of my eyes.

The crying didn't make me feel better. My tears were hot, and the muscles of my face hurt. But the harder I squeezed my fists, the better I felt. I pressed my fists into the bed, and then I punched the bed as hard as I could, and it felt good. My arms felt strong.

Anger creates energy.

I howled in frustration and punched the bed so hard I could feel the metal bed frame underneath. My voice came out in a guttural yell that scraped my throat raw. I didn't care. I felt powerful in my pain. At the bottom of my rage was one thought that kept looping over and over:

Who will love me? WHO WILL LOVE ME?

You will, whispered the calm, tender voice in my head, and I collapsed onto the bed, exhausted.

One last question filled my mind as I curled into a ball. *How?*

Keep feeling, the tender voice whispered.

I didn't realize that was her answer for me. I kept asking, *How? How? How?* I rocked back and forth until there was no energy left, and then I fell asleep.

I'd blamed my feelings for keeping me stuck in this cycle. But I slowly started to realize it wasn't my feelings that kept me on that figure-eight track. It was my resistance to them. I'd see an emotion coming and sweep away from it around the curve.

I knew that I'd keep going around and around until I stopped to feel.

I just didn't know how to feel one thing without feeling everything at once. My brain would short-circuit into a migraine, I'd take a shitload of ibuprofen, and then I'd feel nothing at all.

24

Shitty Yoga

The more my emotions came through to be felt, the more I felt like a monster. I stopped caring for the monster in the hope she would wither away and leave only the good parts of me behind.

I started pouring twelve- to fifteen-hour days into my job. My work felt like the one area of my life where I could do some things right. The more work I took on, the more work seemed to need doing, and part of me was grateful for a "legitimate" excuse to avoid my partners and my feelings. I focused on emails, manuscripts, and people who needed me but didn't know me well enough to ask how I was doing.

Anytime I stopped working, the emotions I'd pushed away all day flooded in, and I dissolved in tears. Jordan wordlessly cleaned up the dishes I left in the sink. He didn't complain when I barely spoke or when I woke him up at night because I couldn't get comfortable enough to fall asleep.

When any text lit up my phone, a flash of heat shot up my neck. If it was Christine saying she still felt angry, I felt like shit. If it was Christine saying something encouraging, like *I know how hard you're working, and I love you and believe in you!* I felt intense shame. I became intolerant of anything nice anyone said about me.

They don't see the real you, Radio K said in his twisted, consoling way. Even answering a simple *How ya doin'?* from a friend required a series of mental gymnastics to respond with some mixture of honesty and optimism. I usually replied that I was busy with work. I felt lonely all the time.

I stopped showering regularly, and I skipped meals. I told myself it was because I had too much work to do, but that was bullshit. I hoped to starve the monster out.

• • •

I started going to yoga every day because it was easier to feel my body than my feelings. I rarely did what the teacher asked. I didn't raise my arms in the warrior poses. I often gave up in the middle of things and lay down on the floor in child's pose, or I just lay on my back listening to everyone breathing hard around me.

My limbs felt so heavy, and I developed all sorts of weird tweaks and pains. Old injuries flared up again, inexplicably. A hamstring tear from eight years earlier started screaming at me when I tried to stretch my legs. An elbow sprain from two years before suddenly made straight-arm poses unstable. My upper back started to spasm again.

I modified most of the poses to make them comfortable, depending on whatever tense muscle or spasm plagued me in the moment. But the pains weren't consistent. One minute I had to protect my hamstring in a leg stretch, and five minutes later I could do a complex pose that required insane hamstring flexibility. My practice looked spastic.

I sometimes wondered why I bothered going to public class at all—but I loved the wood floors of the studio, and the warmth of the room, and the thick incense smoke that made me breathe slower. It felt important to practice shitty yoga in front of other people. Each class proved to me that it didn't matter if my practice looked sloppy or disorganized. Yoga class was the one hour of my day when I did my damnedest to take great care with myself.

And something miraculous happened in those classes: I realized I could feel my emotions in front of other people and not die.

One morning after class finished, we were all politely bumbling over each other to get our shoes and a guy from class turned to me and asked, "Are you injured or something?"

"Emotional injuries," I said.

He didn't laugh. I suppose that's because it wasn't really a joke.

My yoga practice finally broke a pattern I'd been trying to break forever: I finally gave absolutely no shits about how I was performing.

This was not my norm. Every time I'd walked into a yoga class before then, I had always sized myself up a little against the other people in the room. In every single pose, I tried to make the clearest, prettiest, most precise shape possible, and a little needling voice in the back of my head always wondered what other people were thinking about me, whether they admired me, whether I was perfect yet.

There was a benefit to that feeling of being watched and needing to perform: I worked really hard at the poses, and I got way stronger and far more flexible. I learned to breathe well, in part because I didn't want to look like I was struggling.

Over time, I actually started to see in myself what I wanted everyone else to see. I started to see that I was flexible, strong, beautiful, composed.

And yet I was always annoyed that I couldn't turn off my compulsion to wonder whether people were watching me. Sometimes I just wanted to breathe without Radio K in my head saying, *Ooh, do you think anyone is listening to how steady and perfect your breathing is?*

I took my glasses off when I practiced so the world would go fuzzy and I couldn't see myself or anyone clearly. It helped anchor me in how things felt instead of how they looked. But then I also missed seeing myself as beautiful sometimes.

When I dragged myself to class in those awful months of self-punishment, that desire to compete with or be admired by anyone totally disappeared. I was grateful. I felt free, for the first time, to do exactly what felt good in my yoga practice. Maybe it was easy to do shitty yoga in this time because I didn't *want* to see myself as beautiful.

I realized that freedom and pain are right next to each other sometimes.

* * *

I got to work with an amazing clinical psychologist who had given up her private practice in part because she was fed up with the system that required her to diagnose and pathologize her clients.

Dr. Valerie invited me along on a women's retreat she was holding so I could experience her work firsthand.

I was there in a professional capacity, to watch her work so we could plan her book together. I sat in a cushy armchair, furiously scribbling notes. I participated in group shares, but I was carefully vague. There was no way I was going to reveal the mess I'd made of my life to Dr. Valerie or to the roomful of successful entrepreneurs.

But for many parts of the retreat, I didn't need words. Dr. Valerie introduced us to an exercise she called "emotional flossing." The idea was for us to all move through physical expressions of a range of emotions: fear, anger, sadness, comfort, and joy.

She demonstrated for us. As we watched, she looked into the distance and began to take sharp, shallow breaths. She opened her mouth and held the sides of her face as her jaw quivered. She shrieked in fear, and my own heart started beating fast, as if I were watching her in a movie. Part of me was entranced at watching her display of emotion from the safe space of a resort living room, and part of me felt awkward and uncomfortable for watching.

After a few moments, her expression turned to anger. She furrowed her brow, curled her fists, stomped her feet, and screamed. The energy of her expression blew through quickly and she started to cry. I thought of myself, on the bed, crying in frustration until I'd completely exhausted myself.

Dr. Valerie tumbled in slow motion down to the floor, and she started petting her upper arms, holding herself, rocking. Her self-comfort lasted a while, until she started to giggle and then belly laugh, and we all joined in. It seemed the only way to release the strange, fast-moving energy that she had brought into the room.

"Emotions are energy in motion," Dr. Valerie explained quietly as she sat back up and dried her eyes. "It is your mind that assigns 'negative' to your anger and 'positive' to your joy. But what if you could develop a full range of motion in your ability to feel? What if you could experience each of your emotions fully, without building a hierarchy around which ones are acceptable and which ones are not? This exercise is designed to help you practice your range of motion."

I felt my shoulders and my chest get rigid. I realized that the next step was for us to do the exercise, and I didn't want to. I briefly thought about making some excuse, lying about some emergency that would give me a free pass out of the room, but I was too slow. Dr. Valerie motioned for everyone to stand up, and the other women in the room stood up quickly, smiling at each other. I fumbled with clipping my pen to my notebook and stowing them in my bag.

We gathered in a circle, holding hands, and then stepped back until our arms were outstretched. Then Dr. Valerie had us drop hands and turn to face out from the circle. I felt a little relieved when I realized that this far apart, we couldn't see each other when we were facing out. She'd engineered community and privacy at the same time.

"When you're ready, begin with fear. You can think of a memory that evokes fear for you, or you can simply try acting out the motions of fear. It doesn't matter. There is no set time you need to stay in any single emotion. Shift between them any time you're ready."

I couldn't think of a memory. I started by scrunching my face and pulling my shoulders in toward my chest. I pulled my hands back. Somehow, the motions themselves seemed to unlock something in me, and I actually felt afraid. I felt my heart beat faster. Women around the circle shrieked and moaned, and I made a noise too. It got trapped in my throat and came out as a soft yip.

I didn't feel the fear shifting or moving until I heard women around the circle yelling in anger. I latched gratefully on to their energy and tried to act the way I thought they might be acting. I yelled and felt my breath deepen to take in enough air. I stretched my arms out and swung fists at the air. I turned my face up to the ceiling and yelled again. I felt powerful. This emotion felt so foreign and liberating to me that I realized I hadn't let it come up in a very long time.

You're used to directing your anger inward so you can feel a sense of control over it, my gentle inner voice suggested. I realized that felt right. I knew what anger felt like. I just wasn't used to moving it out of me. *You think if you hold it inside of you, you're taking responsibility for it. But that's not what personal responsibility is.*

I couldn't hold the energy of anger for long, and I was one of the first ones to begin crying. I sobbed easily and unabashedly. This emotion was easy and quick to access. I reached down to the floor for support and stayed on all fours for a moment, letting myself cry in heaves.

When I was tired, I lay down and wrapped my arms around myself. The other women were on the floor, too, cooing to themselves. I ran my hands over my own shoulders and waist, and realized I'd never done this for myself before. I'd curled up into a ball after crying plenty of times, but I'd never stopped to hug myself. My own touch was tender and reassuring, and that surprised me after spending so many months beating myself up.

I was grateful for the first woman who started to laugh, because I didn't think I had it in me. I had to fake the laughter at first. But once I heard the other women and felt my own diaphragm bouncing up and down with my lungs, I relaxed into it. The laugher felt good, and when it was over, I breathed a lot easier.

I sat up and looked at everyone. They all had soft, sweet smiles on their faces, their hair mussed from rolling on the floor. *I can feel emotions and not only not die,* I thought, *but I can be accepted.*

The next task, I knew, would be to learn how to feel my emotions with people I was afraid to lose.

. . .

At home, I started to practice feeling.

After Jordan went to work, I put on songs guaranteed to help me cry, and I threw myself around the living room in some mashup of yoga and dance and flailing. I roared in frustration until my throat was hoarse. I didn't care if I lost my voice; I figured I'd drink herbal tea and tell everyone I was coming down with something.

I writhed on the floor crying, and then, when I was all exhausted of tears, I realized how dusty the floor was. I dragged myself up to standing and started vacuuming the whole house.

I think the accurate term for this bizarre one-person sport is "shame wrestling."

I reflect on that now and just think, *Oh, honey. It's okay to feel. It's okay to care for yourself. It's okay to love. You only need to reach out a little bit. Call a friend and leave a voice message. Let them help you prove to yourself that you are lovable.*

I wasn't ready to hear that voice yet.

25

Basement Renovations

I had a dream that I was trying to sneak out of my parents' house in the middle of the night without anyone hearing.

In real life, throughout middle school and high school, I'd tiptoe out of the house all the time when I couldn't sleep. From a young age, I had the overwhelming sense that life was flying by—a side effect of living in a small town was the sense that there was so much more to the world and I'd never see it. Frogs were in the creek learning to mate in the dark, owls were snapping up rodents in the silvery meadow, people in the next town over were working through the night shift; there were so many lives to be lived—and I was going to miss all of it because of something as boring as sleep.

I would sneak out the door and walk through the woods, listening to the sounds of critters running in the leaves and coyotes out in the cow fields. I liked how I felt in the dark, sure-footed even when there was no moon to help me see. Sure enough of myself to forget myself. To let go of the anxiety I felt over having to one day choose a particular kind of life to live, and how my choice would mean the death of everything else that could have been.

In the dream, I moved through the house just like I had as a kid. I skipped the fourth stair, which creaks. Down in the kitchen, I approached the spot in the floorboards that usually lets out a little squeal, and I crawled over the counter to avoid it. But as soon as my hand touched the knob of the back door, I heard a muffled *bump*.

I froze. Surely I'd woken someone, and I was about to have to explain myself. My brain raced to come up with a lie. I didn't want to explain to my parents that I just wanted to go outside and stand under the moon—*because that's a weird thing to do,* Radio K chided. *Something must be wrong with you. What's wrong?* I didn't want to answer that.

How could I explain that I'd made a mess of my relationships, that I felt disconnected and queasy, that I didn't trust myself, that my emotions were all wrong, that I'd made the wrong life from everything that might have been possible?

Better to pretend I felt nothing than to try to describe feelings I was ashamed to explain. *I just came down for a glass of milk,* I could say, though I knew that wouldn't explain why I was crawling on the counter alone in the dark.

But it wasn't my parents coming down from their room. The sound had come from the basement, and I could see light coming from under the door leading down the stairs.

I opened the basement door and looked down the stairwell. A halogen work light on the floor cast orange-yellow stripes up the wall, cut with diagonal shadows. I peeked my head around the corner, and I saw a crew of workers tearing the basement down to the studs.

The soft *bump* that had stopped me in my tracks upstairs came from a woman using a sledgehammer to knock out drywall. Another measured two-by-fours and cut them to length. Half a dozen women moved about the room, handling each task with exacting precision. Despite the commotion, the space was quiet as a library.

The foreman looked up as I came into the room. She'd been bent over a plan she'd scrawled on a spare piece of drywall, but now she straightened up and studied me.

"What's it going to be?" I asked.

She looked around at the women working and then looked back at me with a soft smile. "We'll see."

"Well, why the change?" I pressed.

She gave me a side-eye, as if to say, *Do you need to ask?* But then her face softened again. "It's time for a new blueprint. Some of these walls were interfering with the flow of the space. It'll be more open now."

The woman with the sledge had knocked down all the walls, save for a column that was still intact on one side of the room. The foreman followed my gaze. "That will stay; it's load bearing."

I nodded. "How will this help me with my relationships?"

She shrugged. "Maybe it won't."

I woke up feeling unsettled. *What if I'm putting all this work into fixing myself only to have my relationships crumble anyway?*

The next day, I told Christine about the dream, and she hugged me for a long time. When I pulled back and looked in her face, her eyes were sparkling—with tears or excitement or both, I wasn't sure. "It was all women," she said, more a statement than a question.

"Yes," I replied, confused.

"And they were renovating your childhood home."

"Yes," I said again.

Christine took a deep breath. "In dreams, a house usually represents your body and mind." I gave her a dumb nod while she looked at me with eyebrows raised and a little goofy smile.

"And they were working on the *basement*," she added, "which might represent your subconscious."

"I don't understand," I said truthfully. I felt stupid. I understood the puzzle pieces; I just couldn't put the picture together.

"Your system might be trying to tell you there are some deep changes happening in your foundation."

Christine leaned toward me, as if to say, *Do you get it now?*

"But I don't feel like things are changing," I said. I felt frustrated. "I still feel so confused and upset."

"How did you feel in the dream?" Christine asked.

"I felt—" I tried to remember. I closed my eyes and took a breath. "Calm. I felt calm, and even comforted. I felt like they knew what they were doing down there." I remembered the foreman's tender expression. *All the people in your dreams are you.*

Then I realized: maybe, even as I cried in public and threw fits while no one was looking, some part of me was comforted, and calm, and knew what to do. Maybe something integral was shifting at the bottom of me.

"I felt like these women were supporting me, were doing the work for me. Like maybe I don't have to work so hard."

Christine was nodding.

It was a revolutionary thought. Maybe I could accept that I lied to Christine and hid from myself, and I could let go of trying to punish myself or force myself to be different. Maybe my desires and my flaws were real and part of what made me human.

For a sliver of a moment, I felt compassion for myself. *Loving and accepting all parts of myself is the way to truly loving others.*

I didn't have enough time to fully process this thought before the moment passed, as though a door had cracked open for a split second and then snapped shut because the light was too bright.

It took me a long time to understand what was happening in the basement. My shame—around my attraction to women, my sexual expression, my deep sensitivity—grappled with my sense that time was always running out on my life. It was just as intolerable to explore my secret desires as it was to never realize them in this one wild and precious life.

To solve this dichotomy, I compartmentalized. I built walls, locked each desire in its own room, and refused to open the door until it made so much noise that I made an impulsive decision one day to throw open the door and let the desire run free, without preparing anyone for what was coming.

I realized the problem wasn't the desires I'd locked in the rooms of my house; it was that I never took a look at them. I'd tried to make all the fearful, confused, insecure, lustful, shy, awkward, slutty, hungry parts of myself disappear behind their many doors. When I shut all of them away, I had very little left to be myself.

Maybe keeping secrets is human. So is telling my truth.

I wasn't so afraid to see myself anymore.

26

Love Made Visible

A ding sounded from my phone. It was Christine telling me she was on her way. She was coming to pick me up for a three-hour-long meditation workshop. "This will be good for us," she'd said. "I think it will help us feel more connected." I was nervous. Three hours of looking into each other's eyes felt like a bit too much for me.

A moment later, Jordan's phone dinged on the counter of our Austin kitchen. "Oh, I'm spending the day with Eve," he told me. "She's on her way over."

Shit.

Christine still bristled every time Eve's name came up. Every time Christine saw a trace of Eve, she said, *She's just everywhere—I need a break from this.*

I told Christine that Jordan had invited Eve over to meet up, and I suggested we meet at the nearby coffee shop instead. She agreed.

Then I got a text from Eve saying she was stopping for coffee on her way to meet Jordan. Did I want anything?

Shit, shit, shit.

I texted Christine again, and she asked to meet on a random street in the neighborhood. We decided to leave one car and drive together.

I hated this avoidance dance. But I went through the steps because I still hated seeing Christine's anger, still struggled to witness her feelings. I was just barely starting to learn my own.

When I pulled up to the spot where we'd agreed to meet, there was a Vespa parked at the curb that looked just like Eve's. For a moment I felt a surge of panic.

It wasn't hers.

You can't protect Christine from what she doesn't want to see. You don't need to change this situation any more for her.

I took a deep breath.

I watched in the rearview as Christine parked her Bronco and walked up to my passenger door. I couldn't tell if she noticed the Vespa. She'd seen Eve's on the street outside our apartment once before, when Eve had come by to hang out with Jordan. My palms started to sweat. My skin was crawling.

Taking responsibility for Christine's emotions felt like a compulsion. I didn't want to do it anymore, but I was still terrified she would stop loving me if I didn't.

I sat for a moment before starting the car. I took a deep breath. I let myself feel my neediness, my loneliness, and I let those feelings go.

Then I turned to Christine. "I don't want to go to the meditation workshop," I said. "I'm feeling really uncomfortable. I haven't felt like myself in months. I've been anxious all the time. I just don't think sitting in silence is the right thing for me right now."

Christine looked down at her nails. "I was really looking forward to this," she said quietly.

I felt another surge of panic. "This morning has just felt so weird," I said. "She's part of Jordan's life, which makes her part of mine. I don't want to tiptoe around forever. I'm interested in dating her again. Not anytime soon. But I need to see that you're working on the pain you feel about this."

Christine started to cry. "That was not a helpful thing to say," she said.

My shoulders felt incredibly heavy, my breathing labored. Even though I felt awful, I didn't feel panicked anymore. "I understand that. I needed to say it," I said, and that felt true even if it wasn't helpful.

Christine sobbed harder, curling into herself until she was pressing her forehead against the dash. I reached over to hug her, and she shoved my arms away.

"Don't touch me. If you're leaving me—"

"I'm not leaving you," I said. But I could feel something had shifted. I didn't reach back over to her. She didn't ask me to hold her tighter.

"I just...it's been months of this, and I wish my desire to see Eve had gone away, but it hasn't." Out of the corner of my eye, I saw Christine raise her shoulders, like she was bracing for an impact. "I feel anxious all the time, anxious about how to be around you, and I—" I choked back a huge wave of shame.

You shouldn't want any of this, Radio K said. *Who do you think you are? You shouldn't be saying any of this.*

It's the truth, the tender voice countered. *The truth isn't shameful. It just is.*

"I can't take it for much longer," I continued. "I love you and I want you in my life. I want her in my life too. And I need things to start shifting around that."

Christine raised her head, but she didn't look at me. She looked straight ahead out of the windshield. "I'm trying to make enough space to feel okay about it. I just need space. I need time."

We've had time, I thought. I didn't say it. We sat in silence for a few moments.

Then Christine squeezed her eyes shut and yelled, "You can have *everything* you want!"

My heart clenched into a stone. I had no idea what she meant by that, but I didn't ask. I was afraid of her anger; afraid I would lose myself again if we talked more about it. I was afraid I would back out and try to appease her again.

I cracked the door to get some air. Christine stayed curled against the passenger door, as far away from me as possible. Her face was buried in her arm. I held the steering wheel tightly in my hands, which was useless, because we clearly weren't going anywhere.

We didn't go to the meditation workshop that day. I felt strange on the short, ridiculous drive alone back to my house. I hadn't thrown myself into the task of making Christine feel better. Instead, I'd said the imperfect, unhelpful things that were on my mind, and when Christine felt hurt, I hadn't taken them back. Because they felt true for me.

And "true" was starting to feel better than "good."

* * *

A week after the failed meditation workshop, when I saw Christine for our date, her face looked more relaxed, more settled.

"I reached out to Eve," she said.

I froze. She looked happy, but I wasn't sure I knew how to read her happiness anymore.

"I started texting her. I just wanted to get a sense of what she was like and to get to know her a little."

My brain cast around for something, anything, to say. "How's that going?"

"We're going to meet up for drinks on Wednesday, just the two of us."

A surge of happiness blazed through me, and I wasn't sure it was appropriate to let it show. Alongside it was a little terror, and guilt, and sadness. I knew how big a step this was for Christine, to go from dreading hearing Eve's name to meeting her face-to-face. I felt guilty for pushing her so hard to take this step. I felt terrified that we might still get so close to everything working out and that it still might not work out. And I felt sad because sadness seemed to underly everything now that I was beginning to pay attention to my emotions.

I had no idea what might be showing on my face or whether Christine could read all that. My mind went blank. I just sat there.

"I reached out to her a while ago," Christine said, "and I didn't tell you. I needed it to be my own thing, just for me."

I nodded, and I suddenly understood. *That's what she'd meant when she said I could have everything I wanted.* My cheeks flushed hot with shame. She'd been doing the work to get herself there, and she needed me to not influence it.

When Wednesday rolled around, I was a nervous wreck. Jordan was going out with a friend that night, and I was going to be alone for the evening. All day I ticked the hours off, counting down to when Christine and Eve would meet up. I wondered if they would smile at each other, if they would get along, if they would talk about me.

I can tell you exactly how this will go, Radio K offered. I listened to him, because I was desperate for anyone to be able to predict the future, even if he was going to be a dick about it. *They're going to have one drink and get loosened up, and they'll start laughing, and they'll realize they actually enjoy each other's company. Then, two drinks in, they'll start sharing more intimate details about themselves. They'll start talking about you and how frustrated they've each been with you. They'll bond over their shared misery. By drink three, they'll realize you are way too much drama, you're not worth it, and not only are they better off without you, but they're grateful this horrible mess brought them together so they can be best friends or lovers or whatever the hell they want, and it will be way less stressful without you.*

I woke up when Jordan came in the room, but I felt so awful I would have sworn I hadn't slept. I reached over for my phone while he pulled his wallet and keys out of his pockets and set them on the dresser. No messages from Christine or Eve, though they'd met up three hours ago. Jordan sat on the edge of the bed next to me.

"How are you doing, sweetie?" he asked.

I burrowed into the pillow. "I feel really uncomfortable."

He crawled under the covers and pulled my body in as close as possible. "In what way?"

"I know Christine and Eve are meeting up to get a sense of each other and make this whole situation easier, and I so admire that. I just keep replaying all the mistakes I've made in my mind, and I'm still so ashamed of myself. I don't feel like I deserve all the effort they're both putting into being in a relationship with me."

"Everything is going to be fine," he said. I wanted to believe him. "I love you," he said.

I burst into tears. I pulled my knees into my chest and he wrapped as much of himself around me as he could, holding me in a tight ball, and I fell asleep like that.

• • •

In the morning, I reached over for my phone, where there was a text from Eve saying the evening went very well and she would leave it to Christine to tell me about it. *Just know you are really, really loved.*

I broke down in silent tears that shook the bed. Jordan woke up to the shaking. "What's up, buttercup?" he said tenderly, wrapping an arm around me again. I told him about the text.

"I don't understand why people love me this much," I said.

By which I meant, I didn't know how to love myself as much as I saw people loving me.

Suddenly, I was seeing all that love in front of me. It was in Jordan's embrace, and in Christine and Eve's meeting, and in everyone's words. Seeing that love was painful because I finally understood: I was the one not letting that love in.

When I first started practicing yoga, the teacher would tell the class to engage the muscles alongside our shins, and I didn't have any idea how to do it. I'd listen to the command and imagine what that might feel like in my leg. I'd touch my leg and flex my foot around and try clenching all the muscles in my leg I could think of until I could feel the muscle the teacher was talking about. It took a long time and a lot of repetition. And then, finally, one day I was able to feel that single muscle and move it, and the whole pose changed.

Maybe self-love is like that. I imagined what it would feel like to actually accept myself, fully accept my desire, fully release the guilt I felt around these memories, forgive myself. Those were the muscles around my self-love. Self-love, liberation, and forgiveness were already inside me always. I didn't notice them until I started to look for how they showed up.

It takes practice to turn your attention to what you want to see in yourself, that gentle inner voice whispered. *You are practicing, and you are beginning to see it.*

At least, at that moment, I was able to notice when I wasn't paying attention to my own love. I believed Radio K less and less. I listened for a softer, loving voice that was always there to take his place.

Sometimes it was Jordan's voice.

Sometimes it was my therapist's.

Sometimes—the best times—it was mine.

27

Holding Hands against the Ocean

"Eve is in the hospital." Jordan's face was pale, his eyes wide. He held his phone out in his hand as if he was unsure what to do with it.

We'd been getting ready for bed when Jordan got the phone call. I could hear him in the other room, but I couldn't make out what he was saying. His voice had sounded strained and higher pitched than normal.

"That was Alex. She and Eve were making dinner at Eve's place. They left the stove unattended for a minute, and it started a fire in the kitchen. It sounds like Eve got really badly burned trying to put it out." Jordan seemed rattled and confused. "She's in the hospital. She might need a skin graft."

He stared at his phone. I put a hand on his shoulder. "Let's go," I said.

"I don't even know what to bring."

"It's okay," I said. "I'll drive. Let's just get there, and if anyone needs anything, I can go."

Jordan nodded. We got in the car.

When we got to the hospital, I looked down at my phone as I was unbuckling my seatbelt.

There were three texts from Christine. She'd been at a dinner with her ex that night, and things had apparently exploded into a fight. Christine was upset and turning to me for comfort.

I typed back a message that I hoped said the right things but still felt lame to me. *I'm so sorry that's happening! Sending you love, honey. I wish I could be there to give you a big hug and kisses. Eve's been badly burned and Jordan and I are at the ER with her. I'll try to give you a call if there's downtime and we're waiting around.*

I felt sick sending it. *Think she'll hate that you're with Eve instead of with her right now?* Radio K teased.

Christine's pain is not yours, my soft inner voice reminded me. I didn't quite believe her, but a glimmer of her message got through to me. I shoved my phone in my bag and followed Jordan into the hospital ward.

The nurse had already given Eve the maximum doses of pain-killers, but they seemed to have barely dulled the edge of her pain. Jordan sat in the chair closest to the gurney and held her good hand.

While we waited for the staff to take Eve to a surgical suite, Jordan and I both tried to distract her with funny animal videos, but we found them much funnier than Eve did. I pulled up my favorite episodes of *Drunk History*. Eve still didn't laugh, but the story lines seemed to hold her attention for small moments at a time.

I smoothed her hair out of her face, and it felt both right and slightly too intimate because we weren't dating, even though I wished we were.

"That feels good," Eve said. "Please just touch me. I feel a lot better when I'm being touched."

I nodded and looked over to Jordan. He gave a weak smile. I sat next to her with one hand on her leg, and Jordan held his iPad with his free hand, using his thumb to play the next episode. We watched three or four episodes before nurses came in to roll Eve into surgery.

I busied myself with every task I could think of to help. I stepped out into the hall to call Eve's brother and update him on the surgery schedule. I volunteered to go to Eve's apartment and get clothes and a toothbrush and a book. Once I got there, I agonized over what clothes would be comfortable enough, what she'd be able to put on without bending around too much, what she would want to wear.

I called Christine on the way back and got the full story on what had happened on her dinner with her ex.

"I know Eve is going through something awful," she said. "I just also wish you could be here."

As she spoke, I took smooth breaths and tried to ground myself by watching an ash tree wave in the wind under the yellow-green glow of a streetlight.

You are enough in this moment, the gentle inner voice whispered. I felt my heartbeat and swayed a little.

Christine's pain is not your pain. Eve's pain is not your pain. You are okay.

I repeated the mantra the whole time I was on the phone with Christine, and I felt calmer. I spoke in soothing tones and promised to call her the next day. Then I hung up and drove back to the hospital.

After the surgery, the nurses only let one person at a time go in to see Eve. When she asked for me, my cheeks flushed. Jordan was there, and so was her brother. I didn't think she'd ask for me. As soon as I walked into the room, she reached for me with her good arm. I held her hand. I couldn't think of anything to say, and for a second I felt guilty for not knowing how to distract her.

Eve's pain is not your pain.

I didn't understand it at the time, but all the things I wanted to give Eve—compassion, love, comfort, care—I couldn't really fully give to her because I was resisting them in myself. I didn't feel I was worthy of compassion, love, comfort, and care, so I withheld those things from myself. In trying to give those things to Eve, there were only tiny slivers of moments when I felt truly present with her.

Mostly I felt like I was going through the motions.

* * *

That night, Jordan stayed in Eve's hospital room on a pull-out bed. I went back to our Austin apartment and slept for a handful of hours. I brought them breakfast in the morning. Eve didn't eat. She was still under observation for a few hours before they would release her, so I went to the hospital library to find a quiet corner to work.

Christine texted a report on how things were going with her and offered reassuring words for me to pass on to Eve. I thanked her. Her text was so kind, and yet I felt agitated. Christine hadn't written about how she felt, and in the absence of her telling me I filled in the blanks.

How Christine feels is not under your control, my gentle inner voice said. I took a deep breath.

When I came back to Eve's room, a nurse was filling out discharge paperwork. "I can't go home," Eve said, looking up from her phone. "They're going to be renovating the damage at my apartment for a few weeks."

Jordan looked over at me, his eyes tender and just a little glassy. "I told her she could stay with us."

I nodded. "Of course. I'll pull the car around."

In the car alone I texted Christine about the plan. *Are you okay with that?* My hands felt hot.

She wrote back that she knew Eve needed help. I wanted to call her to hear how she felt, but I knew Eve and Jordan would be waiting for me at the entrance.

Your decisions are your own, I told myself. *You can't decide how much to care for Eve based on how Christine feels about it. Follow your heart.*

After we got Eve arranged in the passenger seat, I sat in the back seat of the car, watching Jordan and Eve chat on the way home. I took deep breaths and tried to let go of the guilt. It partly worked.

A few of Eve's friends came by the apartment to hang out and cheer her up while I went on a three-hour mission to get her prescriptions filled. One pharmacy had one of the medications, but they were out of the pain pills.

It was the one prescription that couldn't wait. The night would be torturous for Eve without something strong to dull the pain, and the pharmacy was closing in a matter of minutes.

I paced up and down the "feminine hygiene" aisle, calling two twenty-four-hour pharmacies before I found a third location forty minutes away that had the medication in stock. Then I called the hospital and waited on hold for twenty minutes for the doctor to free up from his last patient and approve the prescription transfer.

From the shelves, maxi pads with wings attempted to flutter off their plastic. *Why do designers always try to make pads into butterflies?* Everything looked stupid. I wandered over to the magazines and stared at the celebrities' faces. The clerk had overheard my half-dozen phone calls and barely contained frustration and seemed not to mind as I picked up three magazines and thumbed through them, not actually reading or caring about other people's drama.

If it took me half the night, I was coming home with the fucking medication before Eve's last dose wore off. I wanted to limit her pain as much as I could.

Finally, the doctor approved the transfer, and I drove out to the pharmacy on the edge of the city. Hours later, when I came back, triumphant, Jordan and Eve and her friends were giggling together in the living room.

"You're finally back!" Eve said when I came in the door, and she held her arms out for a hug. I leaned down to wrap my arms around her. "It took you so long," she said.

"Yeah, I had to drive all over," I said vaguely as I unpacked the medications. I checked the labels to see what she should take and doled out pills from each bottle. "This should help you sleep," I said, handing her a glass of water and the handful of pills.

I set a small glass of prune juice down. Eve wrinkled her nose. "I know," I said. "It's going to taste like shit. But when you're not stopped up and in agony three days from now, you'll thank me."

Her friends were still chatting away, in the middle of some story. Eve grabbed my forearm and looked me in the eye.

"Thank you," she said. "Seriously."

I smiled, nodded, and went to the kitchen to draft out a timetable for Eve's medications. I set an alarm for her next dose.

Jordan set Eve up in our bedroom because she'd have more room to spread out and it was a straight shot to the bathroom. As we all settled in for the night, we remembered that Jordan snored, and Eve couldn't sleep through it. He went to camp out in the guest bedroom. I slept in my bed, with Eve in it.

"Will you hold my hand?" she asked that first night. I knew that just a little bit of touch would soothe her and that she was in a lot of pain. I thought about sea otters, who hold hands while they're sleeping, floating on the ocean, because otherwise they might drift apart from their loved ones. I fell asleep holding her hand.

*   *   *

The next day, Christine offered to come over and help Eve with a legal issue with her landlord over the fire. I knew Eve and Christine were getting to be on friendly terms, but I was blown away by this act of kindness.

Christine asked to spend a little while alone with Eve to chat, so when Christine showed up, I gave her a kiss, and then I got in my van and drove robotically to Target, which was stupid because

I hate Target. The fluorescent lights seem to beam at the frequency of anxiety, the store's signature red color the glaring red of an alarm. I took a big cart and roamed the whole perimeter of the store until I got to the labyrinth of paper products. I bought a twenty-four-pack of toilet paper even though Jordan and I would likely head back to Tucson before we ran out.

I got back an hour later, and Christine and Eve were still chatting behind the closed door of the bedroom. I went back out to the sidewalk and stared at the train tracks.

Christine came out and I stood up to give her a hug. "It's really amazing you came to help Eve. Thank you. How are you?" I asked.

She shrugged and gave a half-smile. Her eyelids fluttered a tiny bit when she blinked. "I'm okay." She ran her hand up the back of her pixie cut and sighed. "I just feel kind of cracked open lately. Like I'm trying to find shelter."

I hugged her again, and she held on tight. A little sob threatened to come out of my mouth, but I stopped the sound. I hoped Christine couldn't feel my ribs flinch.

Christine feels cracked open because you're the one who did the cracking, Radio K whispered. *And she knows you can't shelter her.*

I projected all my worst judgments of myself onto Christine. *She sees how limited you are. You are not enough.*

Christine pulled away and said she needed to get to work and couldn't stay. I nodded, thanked her, and walked her to the front door. I watched Christine drive away, and I stayed out on the front porch alone for a few moments, checking in with myself.

The truth was, I didn't trust myself. It wasn't enough to me to show love and care the way I wanted to. I needed approval from

Christine and Eve and Jordan to feel I was doing the right thing—as if there was some "right" thing to do in an unprecedented situation like this. I was so tired, and I was upset with myself for feeling tired.

It's okay to feel exhausted, my quiet voice piped up. *You've all been through a lot. Let yourself rest.*

I found myself nodding, my eyes tracing the train tracks.

You are enough. Give yourself the love you need. When you're ready to truly care for yourself, you'll be able to see how much you have to give.

I wiped away tears and went inside. Eve was napping. I knew I only had a short window to get work done before the next errand needed to be run.

Two weeks later, Eve's apartment was ready for her. When she moved out, I finally let myself feel how tired I was.

I let myself feel tender, too. I thought about how sweet it had been to fall asleep holding her hand, and I missed her.

28

Out in Public

Work wrapped up in Austin, and Jordan and I packed the van back up with the few things we'd brought. We rolled through the blank open stretches of western Texas listening to podcasts, pausing the show for hours-long discussions sparked by what we'd heard. The drive was simple and easy. I missed simple and easy, even as it was happening. I wanted to stay in this blank space with nothing to do.

As soon as we got back, Jordan's parents were about to leave Tucson for a months-long trip to their cabin in Minnesota, and Jordan invited them to come have dinner with him and me at a downtown restaurant the night before they took off. He was fidgety and agitated as he sent off the text. I asked what was up.

"I want to tell them about Eve," he said. "Are you okay with that? I know it's basically outing you too."

I felt a tiny flutter of panic under my skin. My track record with talking to my own parents hadn't been so great. I hadn't talked to either of my parents about Christine or Eve since that first disastrous conversation with my mom.

But I felt a surge of pride that Jordan was ready to talk to his parents. The more I could stop filtering myself around the people in my life, the better.

I nodded. "I think that's really great. How do you feel about it?"

He looked a little stricken. "I'm nervous."

I nodded. "Sounds about right."

When the night of the dinner came, I was way more nervous about it than I'd expected to be. I kept flashing back to how tongue-tied and stupid I'd felt trying to talk to my mom. *We were going to be in a public place; was that a good idea or a bad idea? What if one of us freaked out? Or got super stony and pissed and made the waiters uncomfortable?* I tried not to analyze it too much.

We went through all of dinner making small talk about his parents' upcoming trip and the rigamarole of taking their dogs in a camping trailer. We cleaned our plates, the waiters took all the dishes away, and all of us finished the last of our drinks. Jordan ordered another beer, and then he got up to go to the bathroom.

I immediately realized: he was buying time. I suddenly felt very uneasy. Here we were, on the edge of the cliff. He was going to say the words, and then they'd be out, and who knows what would happen next.

I fidgeted in my chair and considered ordering a beer for myself, but I didn't. Jordan's parents looked disinterestedly up at the TV mounted above the bar. It was playing *Honey, I Shrunk the Kids.* The waitress came by and set Jordan's beer down on the table, and the foam ran down the sides of the glass.

Jordan came back and sat down, and his parents turned back around to look at him.

"So, this feels kind of awkward to bring up, but it doesn't come up naturally in conversation," Jordan began. He swirled his pint glass in the ring of foam on the table. "Emily and I have an open relationship, and I'm dating a woman named Eve."

"I'm dating someone too," I added. "Her name is Christine. They both live in Austin."

Jordan and I looked at his parents expectantly.

Jordan's dad nodded first, looking at me. "I might've guessed something like that," he said. His voice was friendly, and he smiled a little. I sat back in my chair.

Jordan's mom was beaming at us. "Well, I think that's just great," she said. "I'm excited to meet both of them someday soon."

Jordan squeezed my hand under the table. I was relieved, happy even. And maybe more than a little bit jealous that the conversation had been so simple. Jordan slammed the rest of his beer and then explained how he'd ordered it to buy time because he'd been procrastinating about saying it. *I knew it.* We all stood and awkwardly shuffled around our chairs and hugged.

As we filed out the door, Jordan's mom touched my shoulder. "I just so look up to you," she said. She hugged me again, and I blinked back tears.

For a moment I saw myself through her eyes, as someone brave enough to love people in the way she wanted to, however messy and imperfect it was.

I was proud of that for the first time.

29

Reunited, Split Apart

When Eve recovered enough to get her normal lifestyle back, she and Christine started hanging out once a week at the pool in Eve's apartment complex.

"That sounds like fun," I told Christine over the phone when she described an afternoon they'd spent together drinking mimosas and floating on the water. I felt a little jealous. I knew it was important for them to have their own sense of each other. But if things were starting to feel easy between them, I wanted to see that. It would alleviate my own nerves.

"I'd love to join you two in a few weeks when I'm in town," I added.

"Okay," was all Christine said.

I felt ashamed for asking. The crawling feeling of anxiety crept up my arms and neck as I remembered Christine yelling in my car,

You can have everything you want! I thought I was being impatient, greedy, immature.

Now I understand that I was judging myself in order to explain my feelings of hurt to myself. I felt angry with Christine and Eve for excluding me. I wouldn't let myself feel that anger for so many reasons—because my relationship with Christine was still shaky and I wanted her to love me, because I was still punishing myself for hiding Eve—and because my anger was unacceptable, I transmuted it into self-judgment.

By judging myself, I could pull away from Christine and Eve, stew in my thoughts, and never have to examine the hurt I felt when they pulled away from me. I took a deep breath, slowly, so Christine couldn't hear it over the phone.

"I'm feeling better and more connected to you," Christine said. "And I'm okay with you seeing Eve again, if you want to."

I didn't respond at first. I didn't want her to hear how excited I was, because I didn't know how to explain it wasn't just about seeing Eve. In my mind, Christine's permission was a concrete sign she was willing to trust me again. It was proof some part of our relationship had healed.

I felt triumphant then. Looking back now, I feel sad. I want to go back and say to my former self in that gentle, tender voice, *Oh, honey. You were waiting for Christine, but you didn't realize you're the only one who gives yourself permission to love the way you want to. In this moment where you get what you want, you don't realize it will take some time yet to get what you need—to love yourself the way you need.*

I wouldn't have listened. I was busy outsourcing my love. For this moment in time, it seemed to work.

"I think Eve is hot," Christine added. "I fantasize about you kissing her."

I smiled. I felt sexy and powerful. The woman everyone wanted.

Even I wanted to be in my own skin that night. When Jordan and I went out to dinner, I enjoyed watching a stranger's eyes trace my thighs in my tight skirt.

Christine and Eve kept swimming together each week. Sometimes it was Eve who told me they'd hung out; other times it was Christine. No one ended up inviting me to the pool.

I resented that, but I didn't bring it up again.

. . .

That weekend, I'd planned a backpacking trip in Big Bend with a friend. On a whim, Jordan decided to hop in the van to meet Eve there for the weekend, a little over midway between our places. We all decided to pitch in together on a house rental the first night, before my friend and I headed into the wilderness.

That evening, we met up at a restaurant for dinner and then went back to the house. We all split a bottle of wine, and Jordan and I played music together, he on his mandolin, I on my guitar. I felt more relaxed and more present in the moment than I'd been in a long time.

It was a two-bedroom house patched together out of a double-wide trailer. My backpacking partner took one of the bedrooms. I started unfolding the couch bed in the living room for myself when Jordan suggested he sleep in the living room so he wouldn't disturb anyone with his snoring. Eve and I agreed to share the bed in the other room.

I felt nervous while brushing my teeth. I hadn't talked to Eve since my conversation with Christine. There was so much to talk about when it came to restarting our relationship and what it might look like the second time around.

Everyone else went to bed and turned out the lights. I was the last one up. I shut the door slowly and went to my side of the bed. Moonlight was streaming in the window, bright enough that I could see the soft smile on Eve's face.

"Christine told me this week that she felt okay about us dating," I said as I got under the covers.

Eve nodded. "She told me. I was waiting for her to tell you before I talked to you about it."

"I'd like to date you again," I said.

"Me too."

Simultaneously, we moved toward each other and kissed. I buried my fingers in the hair at the back of her head and slid my other hand across her back. She was wearing a crop top to sleep in, and I was grateful for it because I wanted to feel her skin but I wasn't comfortable yet reaching under her clothes.

She slipped her hand under my shirt.

I pulled back. "I want to take this slow. I'd like to have a date with you when we get back and talk about what we each want in a relationship together. I want to talk about that before we sleep together. Is it okay to just make out?"

She nodded. "Is it okay to touch above the waist?"

A little flush of energy rolled through me, a weird mix of tension and excitement and embarrassment, and I giggled a little. "Yes," I said. Then I reached for her again and planted my mouth on hers.

She grabbed my breast and pulled me in close until I could feel her belly pressing against mine. I opened my eyes just enough to see the silver shape of her neck and cheek in the moonlight. I felt lightheaded.

"Fuck it," I whispered, and leaned back to pull off my clothes. Eve pulled off hers.

. . .

After the Big Bend trip, Eve followed us back to Tucson. The first night having sex with Jordan and Eve together was the most free and uninhibited I'd felt in a long time. My brain stopped whirring for a while and I relaxed into my body, letting myself move the ways I wanted to move. The doubt and anxiety that had dogged me the last several months melted away. I didn't worry whether I was doing the right thing or the wrong thing. I let myself be.

But always too soon, I was back on a plane or in a car between Tucson and Austin, and then I was unpacking my suitcase in a familiar-but-neglected bedroom, and when I wasn't on a date night with one of my three partners, I felt strung tight like a piano wire.

I'd gotten a temporary high from being back with Eve, and a temporary sense of relief from Christine's blessing. I felt lighter and more playful around Jordan. All these parts of my life were beautiful, but the only times I felt good were when my partners felt good. I still leaned on their emotional states as a barometer for my own self-worth.

. . .

One night when Eve was still in town, we were sitting on the couch smiling at each other, and Jordan asked, "Do you want to have sex?" Eve smiled wide and nodded enthusiastically. My body went stiff, and then I panicked a little. I didn't want to withdraw, so I nodded and said I needed to go to the bathroom.

I sat on the toilet lid and took a few deep breaths, fighting with my thoughts. *They're both so hot. You always have a good time. Why are you hesitating? Why are you sabotaging this?*

But since I was bullying myself, I didn't stop to listen for answers. I didn't listen when the quiet, gentle voice in my head was saying, *You don't feel worthy enough to consider what you actually want, but you are. Stop and listen to yourself. The anxiety you feel right now isn't about having sex or not having sex; it's about feeling worthy if you say yes and feeling worthy if you say no.*

I didn't stop to listen. Instead, I told myself to get it together. I pulled my T-shirt over my head as I walked into the bedroom.

Suddenly I was hyper-aware of every sensation. My ears buzzed. The bedside lamp was glaring in my eyes, so I turned away from it. My lovers' hands grabbed at my remaining clothes, grabbed at my skin, pulled my face in closer to theirs, and my body was humming with resistance. Fingers felt like sandpaper.

It wasn't that I didn't want them to touch me. It was that I wanted to want them to touch me. And I hated myself for feeling differently.

When I'd stripped down to my underwear, I kneeled on the bed and put my hands on each of their shoulders so they would stop and look up at me. "I'm so sorry," I said, "I just—I'm not quite there yet. Or not quite here, in my body. I'm feeling really distracted. Could I watch you two for a little bit instead?"

They both smiled, nodded, and crawled toward each other. I lay back and smoothed my own hands over my belly, breasts, thighs, neck. I loved watching them make out, loved watching how each of them responded to the other's touch. I slid my fingers under the edge of my underwear. I reached my other hand over to gently pull Eve's hair, and she moaned and threw her head back.

I started to relax, knowing I could choose to join when I wanted to. In just a few minutes, my desire roared back and I crawled over to help Eve come. When they turned their attention on me, I let go of all the thoughts in my head and the tension in my back. As I came, I felt a surge of energy rush up my spine, surround my skull, and burst—and immediately afterward, I broke into heaving sobs.

"What's wrong?" Jordan asked as Eve lay down next to me.

"I don't know," I said, rocking myself side to side. "I just feel really overwhelmed."

Eve and Jordan both wrapped their arms around me. "You let go," Eve said. "That was beautiful."

• • •

The next time I was in Austin, Christine and I were supposed to have a date night, but she texted me in the afternoon asking if I could come to her place beforehand to talk.

After the whiplash afternoon where she'd asked me to come to her office and I'd broken down in tears when she said she thought everything would be okay, she'd changed her approach when she needed to talk about something. Usually if she wanted me to call her right away, she would add *it's good!*

There was no *it's good* this time.

As I drove over to her house, my whole back felt rigid and tense. Panic rose up my rib cage and I tried to shove it down. *You don't know what she's feeling or what she needs to say,* I told myself. *Stop assuming she's going to break up with you just because you still feel guilty.*

Christine's face was tense when I showed up. She smiled only halfway in greeting. We settled into her couch, and she said, "I need to take a break."

For months I'd carried around anxiety that at any moment Christine might say those words to me—or worse, that she would say she needed to break up. Despite my fear, I hadn't expected her to ask for a break on this day.

We'd made it through the worst in our relationship, I told myself, and things had just started to feel easy between us again. She didn't ask for a break when she was feeling heartbroken and distrustful of me.

Why now? My mind reeled. I stared at Christine with my mouth half open.

"You haven't done anything wrong," Christine said. "In fact, you've been great. I don't know why I need a break right now. I can just tell something really big and fundamental is shifting for me, and I need some time to myself to go through that."

I nodded. "I'll support you in whatever you need," I said. "Is there anything I can do?"

Christine put her hand on my arm and shook her head.

"How long do you think you want to take?" I asked.

"I don't know." I was about to take a trip with Jordan to go see family in Colorado. "Maybe I'll be ready to connect when you get back," Christine added.

"Do you want to hear from me during this time? Can I still text you?"

Christine thought about that. "Yes, I think it would feel okay to text about what's going on in our days, just not processing stuff between us. Is that okay?"

I nodded and hugged her. "I love you."

"Thank you," she said, and I got up to go. She stayed on the couch as I walked out the door. I waited until I closed the gate behind me to reach up and wipe the tears from my eyes.

In my gut, I knew we wouldn't get back together when I got back from Colorado.

I'd borrowed her love for a while to patch over the hole in my own. And when I sabotaged her trust, I finally uncovered the hole in myself. I could no longer use Christine as a proxy for my own self-worth, my own self-love, and my own inner voice.

I was done fighting my emotions. For the first time, I was beginning to accept how I felt and sit in the truth of my emotions. The truth was, I still felt the strain of a codependent tie to Christine. I still didn't feel okay when she wasn't okay. I didn't know if I would be able to snip that thread and stay in a partnership with her at the same time.

But I was starting to understand that finding steadiness on my own two feet was more important than trying to hang on to her for balance.

I didn't know what would change for Christine in our time apart. But I knew I would keep listening to myself.

30

The Talk, Take Two

A few weeks later, Jordan and I took the road trip up to Colorado to see my extended family. My parents were driving out from Illinois. It was the first time I'd seen them in person since Christmas. Part of me had wanted to talk to my parents about Christine when we were together at Christmas, but it was too daunting to explain that not only did Jordan and I have an open relationship and I was dating women, but I'd made a giant mess of it all.

Dad won't understand you, I convinced myself. *He met Mom in high school and has never been with anyone else. He'll think you're just confused and irresponsible.*

In reality, I had projected my inner doubts onto my dad. I didn't understand myself. I felt confused and irresponsible. And because I hadn't talked openly with anyone in my family about it, I felt really alone when we arrived in Colorado.

Since the car ride with my mom, I'd tried to—not bait her, exactly, but—give an opening to talk about my relationship with Christine in various passive and uber-casual (read: completely loaded but obscure) ways. On phone calls with her, I said things like "I was hanging out with Christine the other day…" or "Christine told me this fascinating thing…"

On phone calls with my dad, Christine was still "my friend Christine." To both my parents, Eve became "our friend who lived with us after her operation."

I was fed up with myself.

When are you going to be honest about who and how you love? I bullied myself with the question. *When it all looks a little happier and tidier, eh?* Radio K chipped in. I shriveled when I thought of telling my parents I had two girlfriends and one of them had asked for a break from me.

What do I want to do here? I asked myself, and I listened for a voice that wasn't Radio K. I knew I wanted to talk to my dad in person, and I knew this trip was my one opportunity until Christmas rolled around again. *I want to tell him.*

Jordan and I stayed with my parents at my aunt and uncle's condo in Colorado. The four of us were in the living room one day, winding down and drinking cider. My dad got up to go to the bathroom, and in the moment of silence that fell between my mom, Jordan, and me, I blurted it out.

"So, I've been trying to find a good time to tell Dad about me being queer." I looked at Jordan. "We are dating a woman together, Eve, and she's really important to both of us. I want to share that. I want to talk to Dad in person, so I thought I'd tell him while we're all here."

My mom's face froze. She'd been looking me in the eye, but her eyes shifted to her drink. "It's not a good time," she said quietly.

We were all listening for the water to run in the bathroom, when we knew my dad would be coming back out.

"He's not doing well right now; he's in a lot of pain because of his shoulder. He's depressed and angry all the time."

I'd known that from my calls with them. Those days, the tone of my dad's voice never seemed to lift. Everything, as he described it, was shitty. Not just his shoulder or the fact that he was in so much pain he wasn't sleeping, but the weather, the job he was working on, the moles tunneling under the grass in his yard.

My mom wrinkled her face in concern, and watching how uncomfortable she was, I felt a surge of empathy. I knew it couldn't be easy for either of them to swim in that energy, gasping for air every day.

I looked down at my nearly empty glass and said, "Okay."

A few seconds later, we heard my dad wrench the handle of the bathroom door open. When he came back in the room, I asked as brightly as I could, "Who wants to go for a walk?"

I couldn't sit anymore. A hot flash of anger crept up under my ears, and I didn't want to feel it. I was angry at my mom for asking me to hide the truth I'd decided to tell. I was even angrier at myself, for abdicating even though I knew what was right for me.

Here you've been patting yourself on the back over how you've learned to listen to yourself, Radio K snickered. *Doesn't take much to push you over, does it?*

It's okay to not be ready, honey, the gentle voice said. *It takes time to know your truth, and it takes time to live your truth. You are learning.*

I was the last to leave, and I took a deep breath as I closed the door behind us.

We all went for a stroll along the creek, talking about the moose Jordan had spotted across the water earlier that day.

I looked down at my feet as I walked through the tall grass by the creek. I almost missed the moose, but Jordan grabbed my arm.

"It's over here," he whispered, and he gently pulled me toward a tree hanging over the water. I looked up, and straight out on the opposite bank was a brown spot with what looked like tan wings.

I gasped. I'd never seen a moose before. My excitement lasted for just half a second before a dull numbness took over.

Stay here in this moment, I thought. *Don't miss the moose.*

But all I could think about was whether I'd ever really feel close to my parents again. *Will you be brave enough to let them in?* I wondered. I felt numb because the question felt too overwhelming to answer.

31

The Millennial Family Portrait

When Jordan and I left Colorado, we drove out to Galveston to meet Eve and her family for the Fourth of July. I was excited they'd invited us along. They'd rented a house within walking distance of the beach, big enough for us as well as Eve's brother and his wife and two kids, and for a week we hung out, doing whatever we wanted.

Eve's parents and I got up early in the mornings to drink coffee and work while Eve and Jordan took walks along the beach. We all hit up funky breweries, getting buzzed and a little too loud, until Eve and her brother shouted at each other at the top of their lungs, arguing about the exact details of some memory from their childhood. We played games at night, staying up so late that I usually curled up on the floor and then finally turned in before anyone else.

Eve's niece, Agnes, was eleven or twelve, and I fell in love with her. She was such a cool kid, excited to do cartwheels, shrewd with cards. She'd never boogie boarded before, so I took her out with me, and we rode wave after wave, breathlessly, until a lifeguard waded out toward us to warn us we were entering a riptide.

Eve's dad, Andrew, told us that at one point he was walking back to the house with Eve's brother and Agnes when Agnes asked him, "Are Jordan and Emily dating Eve?"

Andrew said that Eve's brother fell silent, totally unsure how to answer the question.

"Yes, they're all partners," Andrew told her.

She looked up at him and asked, "How do you feel about that?"

"My daughter is the happiest I've ever seen her," he said, "so I'm really happy."

Andrew told me about this exchange while we were standing in line waiting to order coffee at some tiny, bougie, beach-adjacent coffee shop that sold only pour overs, cold brew, and CBD tonic. Texan moms in white jogger pants were chatting, their giant black sunglasses obscuring most of their faces, and a bearded dude with a Lone Star belt buckle and a designer palm-print tank tapped his phone against the card reader to pay for his eight-dollar coffee.

When Andrew told me how he'd answered Agnes's question, I burst into tears, and I hugged Andrew until his arms loosened and he made it obvious the hug should be over.

It meant so much to me that Andrew would so readily accept all of us and speak so simply about it to his family.

I also cried because I realized I'd not yet been able to show my parents that side of me.

I was so nervous about how they would react to my partner choices, which had turned out so different from theirs, that I hadn't opened up to them about the joy I felt spending my time with them. I hadn't shared the joy I'd felt in taking chances and experimenting with what I wanted my life to look like and whom I wanted to share it with.

At the bottom of it all, I cried because I still needed to hear that it was okay—great, even—to love whom I loved.

I was borrowing Andrew's validation until I was strong enough to build my own.

That night, while everyone crowded on the sand to watch the fireworks across the bay, I waded shin-deep out into the ocean, until the sparks seemed to shower across the water and run into my legs. Agnes joined me out there, and for a moment it was just the two of us.

"You really like Eve and Jordan, huh?" she asked.

I teared up again and nodded.

"Yeah," I said, "they're my family."

Eve and Jordan walked down to join us. The fireworks were blurry in my tears; it was the most spectacular fireworks show I'd ever seen.

32

The First Ending

Back in Austin, I met Christine for coffee. While we'd been apart, we'd texted back and forth every couple of days. She said big things were starting to shift in her life. There was new positive movement in the custody talks with her ex. She had ideas for next steps in her career. She'd reconnected with old friends.

"Some days I feel the best I've ever felt, and other days I get big waves of emotion," she said. I felt a pang of guilt and shame. *Were the big waves of emotion still from what she was processing in her relationship with me?*

You are not the only force in her life, my tender inner voice reminded me. *It's not always about you. You don't create her feelings. They are hers alone.*

I knew it was time to let my shame go. *You do not have to hold on to your relationship with Christine to prove you can be loved.*

As I drove to the coffee shop to meet her, my hands shook on the steering wheel. I wanted her back as a friend, but I needed distance from her as a lover. I needed to steady myself in myself.

I was the first to arrive. I ordered a cappuccino and snagged one of the big cushy couches. The coffee shop was crowded, and I started to kick myself. A noisy café was not where I wanted to have this conversation.

When Christine walked in, my heart leapt. She was still so beautiful to me. I loved how she stood with her shoulders back but relaxed, so self-assured. As soon as she saw me, she gave me a broad, warm smile.

She sat down with her coffee, and we chatted for a while about her new career plans, her family, my trip to Colorado and Galveston.

Once we'd finished our drinks, I looked up. "I have something to talk about with our relationship," I said quietly. Christine nodded and put her warm hand on my knee.

"It's so busy in here," I said, looking around. "Would you be willing to come to my place so we can talk privately?"

"Yeah," Christine said, and she smiled that warm smile again. I didn't feel so nervous, somehow. It was a short drive back to my apartment, and I spent the whole time counting my breaths. I made tea for us, and we settled onto the couch.

"Since we've been apart, I've been thinking about the dynamic of our relationship. I still can't shake feeling awful when you feel awful. I think it's in part because I take on your emotions as my own. I know that's not right, but I don't give myself enough distance in our relationship to stop doing it."

I flicked my eyes up to Christine's face. She was nodding. I took a breath. "The other part is that I unconsciously created this hierarchy between us. I put you on a pedestal above me. I don't think of myself as worthy of you."

Christine's eyes were wide now, but soft and a little glassy with tears. She rested her hand on my shoulder. I gulped another breath. "That's not okay," I said. "I need a bit more distance from you to start unwinding that. I don't want to go back to a romantic relationship with you. I want to just be friends."

Christine broke into a wide smile and tears fell down the sides of her cheeks. "I'm so glad," she said. "I was thinking the same thing." She lurched forward and gave me a strong hug. I started to cry big sobs to relieve the tension I'd been carrying around for the better part of a year.

Christine pulled back and held both my hands. "I'm so excited to be the best of friends."

I felt relieved. Not because Christine felt the same way. Because for the first time, I felt fully like myself in front of her. I wasn't trying on a sexy or spiritual or strong version of me. I was all those things and more.

In getting truly honest, I'd found myself.

33

Stray Wanders Home

A few days later, my entire company gathered in Austin for a summit full of operational updates and personal development sessions. I'd impulsively signed up to deliver a "One Last Talk," based on a book with the same title by Philip McKernan. The premise of the book is: if you were about to die, and you could deliver one message you needed to say to the person who needed to hear it, what would it be?

Four of us had signed up to deliver these talks, and for some godforsaken reason I'd not only agreed to do it—I'd *volunteered*. Gotta love a forcing function for facing your demons.

I'd spent so long convincing myself that being queer and poly-amorous were just details of my sex life and that my parents didn't need to know about my sex life. But these details about me have to do with much more than sex. By editing them out, I was editing out all sorts of details about how I spent my time and who was important to me. I edited out my love for people in my life and how I felt it and what I'd chosen to do about it.

I edited out myself.

So I wrote a talk about how I hadn't come out to my dad yet and how my fear was standing in the way of deepening my relationship with him.

And I prepared to give this talk to my company of forty-five people.

Why on earth would you air your dirty laundry to all those people? Radio K asked.

To which I thought, for the first time, *Who I am and whom I love are not "dirty laundry."*

A shiver ran through me when I thought it, but it wasn't fear or anxiety. I felt powerful. My love was more important than my self-destructive thoughts.

As for coming out to a whole company of people before coming out to my dad, all I can say is that it seemed easier to address a crowd because I didn't have to look anyone in the eye. I didn't care if they judged me. I thought somehow it would be good practice for the more important conversation I needed to have with my dad, who I was terrified might judge me.

The night before the talk, I was nervous as fuck. I couldn't decide whether I needed to be alone or be around people, so I ended up being a pretty loud, obnoxious version of myself. I leapt enthusiastically on any distracting idea—*Let's all swim in the pool! Let's get drinks! Let's do karaoke! Let's invite the Uber driver to karaoke!*—and I was equally grateful when everyone declined. I had a couple of beers, hung around outside until my colleagues' smoking started to make me cough, and went to bed early.

* * *

That night, I had this dream where my mom came to visit me. In the dream I lived in San Francisco, and I was driving my mom around in Jordan's car. I'd never been to San Francisco, but I pictured what I'd seen on TV shows: steep hills, the screech of trolley tracks a few blocks away, Pride flags in apartment windows.

I parked somewhere, and we wandered around twisty-turning blocks looking for the place we wanted to go, and then I realized I didn't put the parking brake on. I had this sense that the car was going to slide down a hill and I needed to go back to stop it. Then I couldn't remember where I'd parked.

My mom and I hunted around the neighborhood, walking around the buildings in a spiral trying to spot Jordan's black car at night. My mom kept finding stray cats and bundling them up in her arms. I kept turning a corner to see Jordan's car rolling backward down a hill. I would run to the end of the block to try to catch it, and then it would be gone.

It must have crashed somewhere, I thought, but we couldn't find the crash.

In the morning, when I woke up from that dream, I immediately thought two things.

The car, I was sure, was some weird representation of the panic I felt about telling my dad I was queer and had a girlfriend. My dad had married the only girlfriend he'd ever had. *Will he be able to understand my decision to step outside a monogamous relationship with Jordan?* I wondered.

I knew that was why it was Jordan's car in the dream, not mine. *Do I fully understand my own decisions? Do they feel like mine?*

In truth, the tangled time with Christine and Eve had felt like a runaway car I was trying to steer to safety. In the last few weeks, since breaking up with Christine, I finally felt like things were slowing down and I was finding my way, even if the lost car in my mind suggested otherwise.

The second, remarkable thing in the dream was that I realized my mom was there with me the whole time. Neither of us knew what to do, but she was *there*. Trying to hold all these cats that kept squirming out of her arms.

And I realized the story I'd been telling myself about this whole thing might be wrong.

I'd told myself that when my mom was quiet after I told her about Christine, when she didn't engage with my offhand name-dropping, it was because she didn't accept that part of me yet.

But what if *I* was the one who hadn't accepted that part of me yet?

I was the one who was being awkward, who was shielding myself, who wasn't engaging. Anytime my mom didn't save me from my own shame spirals, I turned it into a story about how she didn't want to connect with me.

I'd constructed this story when I believed parts of me were unacceptable. I projected my self-judgment onto my mom, to give it a face and to give me a person to rail against.

But in that dream, she was there, holding five stray cats in her arms, following me wherever I needed to go.

. . .

That morning, before the talks started, I took a walk around the house where my colleagues and I were staying. I called my mom.

As we talked, I walked around and around the block of the rented house, staring alternately at my feet, the weeds, and the curb. I probably walked around the same block eight or nine times.

I told her I was on a work trip, and how excited I was to see my colleagues, and how much I loved the culture of my company, where we spent our summits talking about our strengths and obstacles, not just professionally but personally, and how much I always got out of these trips.

"This time, we're doing these speeches," I said. "The idea is to imagine that if you were about to die and had just one last opportunity to speak your truth to someone who needed to hear it, what would you say? And then you build a talk around that message and give it to at least one person. We have a day where a few of us deliver them to everyone in the company."

"That's so cool," my mom said.

"I signed up to do one." I stopped and kicked my toe against the curb. One, two, three, four, five times. My mom waited for me to continue.

"It's about this journey I've been through in coming into my identity as a queer person and about the relationships I've explored and…" I fished around for the best way to say the next part. "And how it's weird, because I've been with Jordan so long that no one questions my relationship or sexual identity. I can just fly under the radar as a straight woman in a relationship with a man, and no one would know these big things have changed for me. And how it feels like such a risk to open up and have these conversations, but at this point it just doesn't feel authentic not to tell the people in my life about this part of myself."

I paused. Stubbed my toe some more. One, two, three, four.

"I've been thinking a lot about that," my mom said.

I looked up suddenly, as if I were expecting to see her on the street in front of me. "You have? I've been wanting to talk to you about it; I just always felt so awkward."

"Yeah," she said, her voice soft and kind. "I haven't known what to say or how to bring it up. It's just so different from anything I've experienced. You know—your dad and I met in high school."

I nodded. "And all the grandparents married young, and then my brother married his high school sweetheart. It's weird being the one in my family who's taken such a different track."

"I think it's great you're exploring what you want," my mom said.

I took a deep breath, and it was just a little shaky, but it felt good. "Part of the talk is about how I haven't told Dad, and I want to."

"You know, I've been worried about how he'll respond. But then I thought about—do you remember, there was this one time at dinner, when you were in high school, and you asked—"

"If he would still love me if I was gay?" I finished. "Yeah, I think about that a lot."

"And remember what he did? He just sat back. He didn't say anything; he just sat there and thought about it."

From some subterranean part of my brain, a new realization came up and smacked me on the forehead. "You're right," I said. "He didn't get mad or anything. He didn't ice me out. He was…fine."

"He took his own time, and he thought about that in his own way, and he was fine," my mom repeated.

"I've been mad at myself for protecting him by not talking about it." The statement popped out of my mouth before I'd thought about it, and I realized it was true. I took a couple of breaths, gently feeling into my anger, and I realized there was more.

The next thing I wanted to say felt risky, but I said it anyway. "I was a little mad at you, too, in Colorado. I know he's been going through his own issues, and I haven't wanted to add to that, but I also just want him to know me. I was mad that we both protected him."

I looked up at the tree canopy above me and took a few more breaths.

My dad does not need protection from the truth of who I am, I thought.

I swear I could hear my mom nodding. She paused for just a little bit. "He might be shocked for just a little bit, but then he'll get over it."

I nodded, kicked the curb, and smiled. "Thanks for talking. I was afraid to bring it all up, and then I had this crazy dream that I'd lost Jordan's car and you and I were wandering around looking for it, and you were picking up all these stray cats…"

My mom laughed. I pictured her face in my mind, head thrown back, mouth open wide enough to see her fillings. I love my mom for that laugh.

"Everything was crazy," I said, "but we were there together. And then I just wanted to call you."

"I love you, beautiful girl," my mom said.

"I love you too, Mom."

34

New Normal

A couple of months later, I still hadn't called my dad.

I was sitting in my therapist's big plush loveseat, shoulders hunched so I sank back into the pillows like a turtle into its shell. I stared into the plastic cup in my hands, watching the lemon wedge and mint leaf floating on the surface of the water.

"I feel like a coward for not having talked to my dad yet," I admitted. "I guess I just assume he'll be confused and upset, because why wouldn't he? It's a pretty non-normative lifestyle to roll out all at once. Not just the being queer part, but having multiple relationships—"

Suddenly my therapist held up her hand, and I stopped mid-sentence. My therapist had never interrupted me before.

She is the most patient person I have ever met. Patience is her superpower. It's how she gets spiraling clients like me to land our own revelations by the end of the hour.

But on this day, she held up her hand and leaned forward. She waited a beat until I took a breath and looked her in the eye.

"It *is* normal," she said.

Then she straightened up, folded her hands in her lap, and stayed silent.

I broke down sobbing.

This had never occurred to me before. *It is normal. I am normal.*

All this bullshit I was projecting onto my dad's reaction—the imaginary reaction he had in my head—wasn't about him or what he thought of me.

It was only ever a reflection of what I thought of myself.

* * *

Jordan and Eve and I drove out to Galveston again to meet Eve's parents and camp by the beach over the long Labor Day weekend. We arrived late at night, which is my favorite time to show up at the ocean.

The first time I saw the ocean was on a road trip my family took to the East Coast. I was eight. I'd fallen asleep in the back seat and woken up to the sound of tires on gravel, then the gentle lurch of my dad pulling the parking brake. It was the middle of the night, but we weren't at the hotel. My dad had driven to the ocean instead. He knew it was more important to touch the ocean for the first time than to get an extra hour of sleep.

Now, any time I drive to the beach, I love to time out the trip so that I arrive at night. I love to go straight to the shore, and even if it's freezing, I pull off my shoes and splash around in the water. I remembered how much my dad loved the ocean and how rarely he'd been there. I wished he was with us. And then I was a little torn, wondering if he'd be able to relax around all of us or if my having two partners would be too weird for him.

I decided, finally, that I needed to know. I was done wondering whether he would accept me. It wasn't a question I could answer on my own. I needed to just tell him.

I still accept myself either way, I thought. *I know how to stay by my own side now.*

The last morning we were at the beach, I woke up before everyone else. I took my phone and a set of headphones down to the ocean, and I started walking. It took me a while to muster up the courage to call my dad; I kept looking out to the horizon, focusing on how calmed I was by the straight line where ocean met sky and divided two shades of blue. I focused on my footsteps, one after the other. I listened to the waves.

Then I dialed my dad.

He picked up. He was working at his woodshop on Labor Day, sanding some cabinets. I could hear the scratch of sandpaper in the background. He could hear the beach around me, and he asked me where I was.

I told him I was on the Texas coast, with Jordan and Eve and Eve's parents.

"And we're here together because…" I paused. I almost let the sentence go unfinished, but then I took a breath. "Because Eve isn't just a friend. She's my partner. And Jordan's partner too. We're here celebrating with her family."

The scratch of the sandpaper stopped on the other end. There was silence for just a moment.

I stopped walking. *I can be okay if he's not okay.*

"Well," my dad said slowly, "I'm very happy for you."

I took a breath, and I looked at the ocean. My dad and I talked for about ten more minutes about other things.

Just before I hung up, my dad said, "I wish the best for you, baby girl. Say hello to Jordan and to Eve."

And I knew everything would be okay, *because I am okay.*

35

The Second Ending

"She won't look at me."

Jordan's eyes were wide. He fidgeted with a button on his shirt cuff, but he wasn't looking at it; he was looking at me, his brow furrowed.

Across the beer garden, Eve had her back to us. She was with a group of friends gathered around hipster table made from a slice of live-edge oak propped on cinder blocks. Eve licked salt off her thumb, threw her head back with a tequila shot, and bit into a slice of lime. She winced and then shook it off by gesturing wildly as she shouted something at one of the friends.

"She's just having fun," I said.

"I think she's avoiding me," Jordan said. "She's been at the other side of the group all night." He'd come out to Austin with me again to see Eve; I could understand he might feel neglected.

"Have you tried going up to her?" I asked, but Jordan's answer was interrupted as a friend came out of the crowd to approach us. When she saw Jordan's face she just smiled, gave a small nod, and walked over to the bar.

"I took a hit of Nat's indica," Jordan said. "I don't think it was a good idea."

"You seem a little paranoid," I said, nodding.

He sighed, and his shoulders suddenly sagged like a marionette whose strings were cut all at once. "I just don't know what to do. I don't know what to think. I mean, do you see that? Do you see that she's been moving away from where I am all night?"

"No, I haven't seen that," I said. "I haven't been paying attention. It's a bar. Everyone's moving around."

He pushed a hand through his hair and grimaced. He looked like he was about to cry. "Am I going crazy?" Then he looked back at my face. "I feel crazy."

"You're not crazy," I told Jordan. "But I don't think you can know whether she's avoiding you unless you ask her."

"I can't ask her about that at a bar."

"Just let it go for now," I said. "Let's just go over there. Try to enjoy the other friends here. You can talk to her tomorrow."

Jordan nodded, and we went over to the table with the tequila shooters. There was a clear spot at the side of the table opposite Eve, and we stood there. Eve didn't look up; her eyes were glued to the person she was talking to.

Jordan gave me that wide-eyed look again. *See?* I just stared back at him, speechless.

What self-destructive loop are you stuck in? I wondered. *Why does it matter so much in this moment whether she will pay attention to you or not? Maybe what you see is true, and she won't look at you—then isn't that just something shitty she's doing right now? And can't you just tell her later that it sucks? Why are you trapped in this?*

My breath was shallow, and I realized I was scared. I saw myself in that rabbit hole. I saw my old beliefs reflected in Jordan's eyes in that moment. *The reason she won't look at me is because I am not worth looking at.*

I stood there in front of Jordan, completely stunned and frozen. I could feel myself getting sucked back into that story. *I am worthless.*

I didn't believe that story anymore, but I didn't know how to fight it off for him. I turned to listen to a story someone was telling about a recent road trip.

On the other side of the table, Eve leaned in to hug a friend and she said goodbye. Then she hugged someone else, straightened up, and turned toward the gate.

"Is she leaving?" Jordan asked. Eve didn't turn around to look our way. I saw Eve go through the passage out to the street and wondered, *Why didn't she look at me?*

I had no answer for Jordan. I shrugged and walked toward the gate. Jordan followed. But outside the beer garden, there was no Eve. I looked to the right toward the bathroom, but the door was open and the light was off; no one there.

"Did you see where Eve went?" I asked a friend who was smoking on the sidewalk.

"I think she left," he said.

"Really?" I said. "That's weird. We came together." Frowning, I headed down the street. Jordan followed.

Eve was around the corner, smoking a cigarette she must have bummed. I'd only ever seen her smoke when she was drunk and pissed at someone.

"What's up?" I asked casually. I wanted my tone to mean, *How's the night been going for you?* But it didn't come out quite chipper enough for that.

Eve raised her eyebrows and flicked ash at the pavement. "What's up with *you?*"

I pointed over my shoulder toward the door. "They thought you'd left."

"Well, I didn't," Eve said, her voice flat. She didn't look at me or Jordan, just dropped her cigarette and smashed her boot into it.

"Is everything okay?" I asked.

"Yeah," Eve said, a bite in her voice.

"Why won't you look me in the face?" I asked.

"Because you two are embarrassing me," Eve said.

"We're *embarrassing* you?" I struggled to keep my voice down. A wave of heat flooded into my stomach and up my neck. My head was spinning far more than seemed reasonable for how sober I was.

"You keep splitting off from the group and going off by yourselves," Eve said. "Other people noticed and asked me about it. I didn't know what to say."

"You keep avoiding me," Jordan cut in. His voice was loud, and he was breathing heavy like he'd just finished a sprint around the block. "You won't even *look* at me."

Eve's shoulders went totally rigid as his voice went up a few decibels. She stared at the car parked next to us. "I'm not going to be able to continue this conversation if you don't lower your voice."

"I'm upset," Jordan said, panting. "You won't look at me; you won't talk to me!" he shouted. Then he took a breath and in a quieter voice said, "I need you to talk to me."

Eve didn't look up, and she didn't say anything. Her face was unreadable in the dark. She kept her head down as she turned and went back to the bar.

Jordan turned after her, but I grabbed his shoulder. "Take a minute."

But just a few moments later, Eve reemerged, talking with a friend as they came out the gate. She didn't break eye contact with the friend as they walked past us.

"Eve." She'd walked past me already, and she didn't turn around when I said her name. I stepped forward toward her. "Where are you going?"

She spun on her heel and faced me. "Danny is going to walk me home."

"That's more than two miles away. Can I give you a ride?"

Eve looked at Jordan standing next to me. "No." She and Danny turned back down the street. Jordan and I watched them go in and out of the streetlights for half a block. Eve didn't look back.

The next day, she texted him to say she had a hard boundary around yelling, and in the past, she'd broken up with anyone who did that.

* * *

Neither of them was able to really talk about it. They were like magnets spun to face each other, constantly repelling. A few months of sporadic travel and a few couples' counseling sessions later, they broke up. We broke up. All at once on that Saturday afternoon, I felt unmoored.

"That's it?" I asked, stunned. "We're over?"

They both looked down. Jordan nodded. I got up abruptly and went out to the back porch to cry. I wasn't sure what this meant for my relationships with each of them. I had no intention of breaking up with either of them; it was their fight, not mine. I didn't like the only picture of my future I could think of in that moment.

I'll have two separate relationships, with separate date nights, text threads, family dinners, vacations…I'll be splitting my time between two separate lives. It was what I had before Jordan started coming with me to Austin, but suddenly it didn't feel right anymore.

Eve came out briefly for a hug. "I'm going to go," she said.

"Are you sure?" I pulled my knees in tight to my chest.

"There's nothing more to say." She smoothed a lock of hair behind my ear. It wasn't hanging in my face. I think she just did it for something to do, some way to show tenderness.

I nodded and bit the inside of my lip so I wouldn't start sobbing. Eve showed herself to the door. I heard the fire door slam on the bottom floor, and her car started up on the street below our apartment window. I heard the engine rev up to the end of our block, and the sound slowly died off as she turned the corner, gone.

. . .

The next day, I thought I felt "fine." I didn't pay attention to how my vision was getting fuzzy on the edges like it always does before a migraine. I was supposed to stay over at Eve's that night. *This cannot happen,* I thought, so I pretended it wasn't happening.

Instead, I distracted myself. I ran errands. I cleaned the apartment. These chores were part of the problem. I equated "taking time for myself" with "taking care of tasks," and these are not the same thing. Running errands to be alone was really just a way to use productivity as a distraction while also lying to myself.

I went to yoga and did the type-A kind of yoga where my breathing was controlled and steady the entire time. I made each shape perfectly, and I was able to do all the advanced poses everyone around the room struggled with, and I felt a tiny bit superior.

And totally full of shit.

I thought I was done with this kind of performance, I thought to myself.

Growth comes in waves, my inner wisdom reminded me. *You're done with this sometimes. Today, you're falling back on it because you're scared.*

With a growing sense of dread, I realized, *I don't want a double life anymore.*

When I got to Eve's place, she'd only just started cooking dried beans for dinner. I knew they would take hours. I was hungry and the migraine was stabbing through my eye socket, but I didn't say anything.

I set my overnight bag in her bedroom, which was strewn with clothes. "Laundry day," she said, sweeping her arm across the bed to pull her clothes into a pile. She dragged a hamper across the floor and started shoving clothes into it.

The bedroom was too chaotic for me, so I went into the kitchen to start making dinner. She'd sent me a recipe earlier that day, and I wanted to feel excited, but I just had a sour feeling in my stomach. I pulled the recipe up on my phone.

I couldn't read it. The letters were all swimming around on the screen. It took me several seconds to piece a single word together. By the time I got a couple of words in a row, I forgot what it was I was reading, like some kind of panic-induced dyslexia.

I don't want to be here in this mess. I wasn't sure whether I meant the mess of our broken triad or the half-renovated, laundry-day messiness of Eve's apartment.

My skin suddenly felt blisteringly hot. I went into Eve's dark guest room, where the tile job on the floor was only half-finished. She'd set a little wire-framed chair in the corner, but there was no cushion on it.

I lay down on the floor, my head awkwardly nestled up to the legs of the chair, and I tried to breathe and feel the cool floor under my back. I started to cry, and tears spilled back to my hairline and trickled into my ears until everything sounded like it was underwater.

At some point Eve stepped into the kitchen and saw I wasn't there, turned the new electric stove off, and found me lying on the floor in the dark.

"I can't cook that," I said. "I can't read. And I can't hear because I cried in my own ears."

She smoothed my hair. "I think that's why most people cry sitting up."

I let out a little half-choked half-laugh and sat up.

"Want to see your surprises?" Eve asked.

"Surprises?"

She nodded. "They're all over the house for you. You found the first one," she said, pointing to the chair. "I know you like to get up early, so I figured this could be your writing space in the mornings."

I lifted myself up and sat in the chair—it was as uncomfortable as I'd feared—and leaned back against the small shearling throw she'd draped over the back.

"And I put in this shelf. We can put a lamp here if you want."

I smiled and said thank you, but I wondered what size lamp would fit on the little floating shelf. There was about enough room for a book and a glass of water.

"And come in here," she said, taking my hand and pulling me into the bathroom. She opened the medicine cabinet above the sink. There was a green toothbrush, and a little tube of toothpaste, a travel-size bottle of my contact solution, and a brightly colored lens case.

"And there's room if you want to bring anything else over," Eve said, and I saw a few inches of space on the shelf before she closed the door.

She led me into the kitchen, to the little table where she usually kept a decorative cutting board and a few cookbooks. She'd replaced them with a French press, a cheap coffee grinder, a bag of locally roasted beans, and two coffee cups. Eve wasn't a coffee drinker.

Next to the coffee cups was a dark striped bromeliad with a striking red bloom. The rest of the plants in her house were always a little starved for water, but this one would be mine.

I cried again, and I hoped Eve assumed they were tears of gratitude. I felt so grateful for her thoughtfulness, and at the same time so guilty over the time and energy she'd spent trying to make her place feel comfortable for me when I still felt so uncomfortable.

"One last place," she said, and led me into the bedroom. We wedged ourselves into the narrow space between her bed and her dresser. She pulled out the second drawer.

"You can keep any clothes you want here," she said, and pulled a little zippered pouch out and handed it to me. It had a flowery screen print of boobs on it, underscored by the words *tiny titty tote*. Inside was a bottle of my allergy medication and a little clip-on reading light. "I want you to stay here from now on when you come to Austin, if you want."

"Thank you," I said, and hugged her for a long time.

We ate blackberries and yogurt for dinner. We went through a bottle of rosé.

"All I want to do is drink," Eve said, "but I never seem to get drunk." It was the closest she got to describing how she was feeling.

She hadn't said anything about the breakup since it had happened. Neither had I. I couldn't think of how to talk about it without wanting her to mend things with Jordan, wanting to go back to a life we could all spend together.

I was willing to talk about the feelings in my body—the migraines, the nausea, the backaches—but I didn't feel comfortable talking about my emotions.

"I can't seem to get tipsy either," I said. "It's a bummer. But I do feel a little numb, which feels better."

As soon as the words came out of my mouth, they felt like a lie. *Does it feel better to feel numb? Sometimes. But sometimes it feels better to feel and to let my feelings move.*

That night, I lay in her bed and stared at the pattern of shadows the streetlight threw on the ceiling as it came through the blinds. I'd stayed at Eve's place so many times, and I'd seen these streaks of light before, but this time I felt the hypervigilance that comes from staying the first night after moving into a new place. I pretended to sleep, but I didn't really.

* * *

Don't cry too loud. Sound leaks through windows. The people inside this apartment will think you're a homeless squatter and they'll call the cops.

Back in Tucson, I went to an outdoor concert by myself, hoping I could clear my head if I was on my own for an evening. The band hadn't started by the time I arrived, so I sat at the bar, drinking a beer, glowering and scribbling in the journal in my lap under the counter.

An hour later, I finally heard someone say, "testing, testing" into a mic, and then, "How are you all doing tonight?" The crowd was so small I couldn't hear their response from the bar. I'd come to get lost in a crowd, to feel anonymous, to dodge attention.

Instead of going into the concert, I got up and woozily steered my bike into an alley. Then I sat down under an apartment window and started bawling. That's when I started worrying the neighbors would call the cops.

I couldn't see through my tears, but I pulled out my journal and started to scrawl things across the page, letting my handwriting get all big and loopy so that I covered a couple of pages in as many sentences.

I hate the logistics of my life right now: the constant text message checking, scheduling every week around travel, trying to sleep in two different places. I still feel uncomfortable at Eve's, and I even feel self-conscious with Jordan. I never know whether to get up out of bed and leave like I want to or stay in bed and cuddle, hoping something in me will soften and I'll feel comforted.

I'm constantly trying to strategize my feelings instead of just feeling them, because I'm worried that something I feel might blow up my whole strategy for how I live. The fuck of it all is that because I love them both, it's shitty to consider what I might want if I were to imagine life with one and not the other.

I don't want to go back to Austin. I don't want to stay in Eve's house. Her ferret smells and leaves hair on everything. I wanted to get drunk so I wouldn't feel like such an asshole, but now I still feel like an asshole.

When the words petered out and I just felt a vague aching numbness, I closed the journal, and then I got back on my bike.

I woke up in the morning with a cracking hangover and a lot of regret, and I immediately judged myself for my behavior the night before. Then I remembered I'd written something important down that I wanted to come back to later. I made coffee and went to my office to look in my journal.

Please don't judge me for messing up these pages. I worry you'll hate me when you see this. I hate myself right now. Please love me in all my messiness and sloppiness and awfulness and self-hatred. I need you to love me, not just pity me, through this. Please don't hate me. I need your compassion right now.

Even my drunk past self feared my sober future judgment enough to write a plea for mercy.

The scrawled words in my journal stung. Not because I thought they were stupid, but because of how afraid of myself I was. I saw, for the first time, how harsh my self-talk could be.

Please don't judge me.

Judge me for what, I knew instantly, even though I hadn't written it down. I wanted to break up with Eve. I thought I shouldn't for so many reasons.

Our triad only just broke up a few weeks ago, I thought. *Don't make any rash decisions.*

You're feeling so emotional right now—do you even trust yourself to know what you need? This question from Radio K snuck in like a wolf in sheep's clothing.

You went through so many months of turmoil with Christine—and it wasn't all about Eve, but it was in part to be with Eve. You want to end this after all that, really?

And then: *You went through so many months of turmoil with Christine—do you really want to stick it out through some more?*

The bald truth was, I was desperate to change what my life looked like. I didn't want all my attention centered around multiple partners anymore. In all this time trying to hold multiple romantic relationships in my life, I'd been in turmoil. I'd pursued relationships hoping to discover that my love would expand to hold more than one person.

But in the past two years, I'd made my life so beautifully, deca- dently, torturously chaotic that I'd pushed out my time to connect with my own self-love. I concerned myself instead with the love of my partners, which, at the time, seemed easier than tapping into my love for myself.

That night, scrawling all over my journal, I knew I was ready for the drama and turmoil to be done. I didn't need Christine or Eve or Jordan to love me in order to hold on to the love they'd each helped me see in myself.

I was ready to let my life be simple, to give myself time to be quiet, to be with myself.

That soft-spoken voice of inner wisdom stepped in.

You don't need to stay in this relationship to prove it was worth it.

36

The Third Ending

"Can we slow down somehow?" I asked Eve on my next trip to Austin. "I'm really struggling. This is a really emotional period, while your breakup with Jordan is so new, and I need more time to just be with myself."

"What do you want that to look like?" Eve asked. Her voice was low and flat. She was watching a fly crawl across the leg of the patio table.

"I'm having trouble sleeping when I stay at your place," I said. I was sure it came as no surprise. Two nights before, I'd gone to sleep long before Eve; she said her brain hadn't wound down enough, and she stayed up watching reruns of *Seinfeld*. I put in earplugs and was deep asleep when she came to bed hours later. She slid under the covers, crawled in close to me, and wrapped her arms around me.

It was only after she'd pulled me in tight that I woke up with a jolt from a dream I was being suffocated. I told her not to touch me. My head spun, trying to map the room and remember where I was.

I felt angry and panicked and deeply ashamed. Eve was trying to comfort herself, and my body had lashed out. I was afraid of sleeping in her bed again, afraid of pushing her away so harshly with no words to explain myself. My body could not get used to sleeping in Eve's house.

"I want to stay in my own place when I come to Austin." I swallowed and watched Eve's face. She didn't look up from the fly. "And I want to go down to one date night for each of my visits. Not that we can't do more if we both realize we want to; I just want to set the expectation at one and see how I feel."

"So roll back to a more casual relationship?" Eve's voice was still monotone.

I shrugged. "I don't think of our relationship as casual. But I think that's the time commitment that would give me space to settle more."

She shook her head. "I don't think I can do that."

Tears started to well up in the corners of my eyes. *Stay connected to yourself,* I pleaded.

"I need something to change. Maybe we could take a break for just a few weeks."

"I don't think I can come back from a second break with you," Eve said quickly. I felt tremendous guilt in that moment, remembering the months we'd stayed friends, stayed on hold, while I tried to heal things with Christine. *It doesn't mean you owe her,* I told myself, but I wasn't convinced.

"Is there anything that would feel good to you?" I asked.

"I don't want to do less than what we're doing right now."

I understood. I knew she was still working through the breakup of our triad, her breakup with Jordan, even though she wasn't talking to me about it. I knew she needed support.

I closed my eyes. *Stay connected to yourself.* "Then we're at an impasse. I don't know what to do."

Eve started to cry. "Are you breaking up with me?"

I felt confused by the question. I wanted to work out something new, but I couldn't think of any other options she hadn't already said no to.

I winced, and tears spilled down my cheeks. "I'm not ready to make that decision. It just seems that neither of us can get what we need from the other right now."

Eve left that afternoon with the conversation unresolved. The next day, she left me a tearful video message, saying if I was going to break up with her, she'd rather I did it sooner than later.

. . .

I sat in my car outside Eve's house for a moment before going in. I had a bag in the front seat of books I'd borrowed and small things she'd left with me. Looking at the bag made me nervous.

I turned the engine off and took a few breaths, looking around at the slant of sunlight across the console. The dappled light bounced in the leaves of the tree in front of her building. I was trying to ground myself in the present moment. *Stay here with yourself,* my inner wisdom repeated over and over. I left the bag in the front seat and locked the car.

Eve didn't come to the door, so I used my key to let myself in. She was in the back, in her bedroom, lying on the bed in a robe watching *Seinfeld* reruns on her laptop. She didn't look up right away when I came in. A few seconds passed before she looked up at me. Her eyes were puffy and ringed in dark circles.

I sat on the bed. She closed her laptop but stayed lying on her side. I took a breath, looked her in the eye, and came right out with it.

"I need to break up," I said slowly. "I've been trying to understand how to live with this split-up lifestyle, but it's not working for me. I'm constantly managing this sense of divided time and divided energy, and I feel really disconnected from myself. We're both suffering a lot, and I don't want to do it anymore."

Eve frowned, and her mouth narrowed to a thin line. "You think we're not worth the struggle? That I'm not worth it?"

My chest felt heavy—not with guilt, but with empathy. I recognized that feeling of unworthiness. "It's not that," I said. "I've been staying in this relationship *because* you're worth it. But this setup is not what I want, and it's not what works for me."

Eve nodded, looking at a spot on her bedspread.

"I'll go," I said.

Then I remembered the bag in the car. "I brought a few things I thought you'd like to have back. I'll bring them in and just leave them in your living room, and then I'll go."

Eve didn't answer. I squeezed her hand and went out to the car. When I came back with the bag, Eve was wandering around the house with a paper grocery bag, gathering up the housewarming gifts she'd bought for me. She was in the bathroom, taking my contact solution and toothbrush out of the cabinet. She handed the bag to me and sat on the bed as I went to the dresser and pulled my pajamas out of the drawer she'd designated for me.

"Can I give you a hug?" I asked when I turned back around. She nodded and reached out for me. We hugged tightly for a long time. When I pulled away, she finally spoke.

"What if we took a break instead of breaking up?"

I didn't answer; I just took a breath, and then another. I could feel my heart beat faster.

"Or we could see each other less," she added. "We could try different things."

My arms went rigid by my sides. I felt confused and angry. "We talked about that already. You said you couldn't do that."

"You can't leave," Eve pleaded. "My family thinks of you as family." She grabbed my arms and hung on to me, and I started breathing faster.

I started gasping. "Why are you offering this *now?*" I felt myself hyperventilating. "I can't—" I stopped myself. *What can't I do? Get through this awful crushing feeling? Rewind to the moments before I said I needed to break up? Make her happy? Make myself happy?* I could feel my pulse pounding in my throat. "I'm panicking," I said.

"Breathe," she said, and she rubbed her palm across my back. I shrank from her touch. "Breathe deeper," she said.

"I need a minute," I nearly shouted, and I stormed out her door. She didn't follow me. I sat on the open-air stairwell with my arms wrapped around my knees, rocking back and forth.

Stay with yourself, my inner wisdom reminded me. I felt the warmth of the sun on my face. My breath started to smooth out.

A small part of me wanted to go back to Eve, to comfort her, to let her comfort me, to take it all back. That was my old familiar pattern. *I'll be okay if you're okay.*

I knew that didn't work for me anymore. This felt better, to sit in the sun, feel my own touch, check in with what felt right for me. To trust the decision I'd made for myself.

I looked up at the tree for a few minutes, watching the leaves wave in the wind. When I felt steady again, I went back inside. "I need to break up," I repeated. I picked up my bag of things and set my key on top of her bookshelf. "I know this is going to take time," I said. "When you're ready to reconnect, I welcome that." I paused at the door for a moment, searching for anything I'd left unsaid. I came up blank. I looked down at the floor, gave a weak smile, and walked out.

The next day, Eve dropped off a grocery sack at my work, handing it to one of my colleagues with no explanation. It was another bundle of things I'd overlooked at her place. Gifts I'd given her that she was giving back. A book of mine she'd borrowed with a love letter I'd written her stuck between the pages as a bookmark.

When I saw the bromeliad peeking out the top, I burst into tears.

37

Take Me Somewhere Beautiful

There was snow on the ground at the trailhead where Jordan dropped me off. I was glad I'd worn my warmer hiking shoes. I pulled on the hat and gloves I'd brought for the overnight low temps.

"Are you sure you still want to do this?" Jordan asked.

"Oh, hell yes," I said. The cold nipped at my nose. I jumped up and down several times to warm myself up in my thin thermal layer. I felt alive.

"You're brave," he said. "It's so cold."

"It feels kinda good," I said, and I meant it. I strapped the pack around my hips and chest. "I'm looking forward to some type-B fun."

"Type-B" was the label we put on adventures that required some suffering to enjoy. Long slogging bushwhacks, bike routes that went uphill forever, climbs that tested each of our abilities to manage our fear.

Trips like that always helped me feel capable and confident when they were done. They helped me remember how to rely on myself.

After my breakup with Eve, I felt more centered than I'd been in a long time—like I'd found my new center for the first time. The drive back to Tucson, usually a slog, felt easy. My heart leapt when the purple outlines of mountains came back into view on the horizon. I canceled the rest of the trips I'd planned to take to Austin that year and arranged to do all my work remotely. I'd never been so happy to see our house. I couldn't remember the last time I let myself relax so much into a hug from Jordan. And before collapsing into bed to sleep for twelve hours, I went outside barefoot and circled the backyard, touching each of the saplings Jordan and I had planted when we first moved in. They were small trees now, silver in the moonlight, so much bigger than the last time I'd stopped to take notice of them. "I missed you," I whispered to each one.

When I finally woke up, mid-day the next day, I pulled out maps of the Santa Catalinas and began to plan a solo backpacking trip. Just an overnight alone, to get deep in the landscape I'd been leaving over and over again for the last three years. I looked forward to a long, quad-burning hike to burn off some of the old emotions I was still carrying around.

I felt ashamed that after so much work getting clear with myself, I still couldn't make my relationships with Christine or Eve work. I had to constantly remind myself that it was because I'd realized those relationships weren't right for me. The shame was the death rattle of my people-pleasing—*you're self-centered and inconsiderate*—but these days, I was shining my attention more and more on that tender, inner voice.

You create everything in your life. You can choose what brings you ease and joy.

I felt residual guilt over keeping the gifts I'd gotten from my relationships with each of them. From Christine, I'd learned practices to check in with myself and take my intuition seriously. From Eve, I'd learned to reconnect with my sensuality and impulsivity.

I'd been drawn to these relationships because I wanted someone to give me a map back to those lost parts of myself. Now that I had found them, they felt like "our" places. I knew it would take time for all the parts of me to feel like they were fully mine.

I gave Jordan one last hug, and he hopped back in the warm car. He waited in the parking lot, engine running, until I'd hiked over the crest of a ridge and I couldn't see him anymore.

It was exhilarating to be on my own. I went exactly as slow and as fast as I liked. I hiked up the ridge, breathing hard, and when I came upon a stand of baby pines, I stopped and sat on a burned log just to look at them for a while. A fire had torn through this area more than a decade earlier. Rumor was that the fire had been started by accident by a woman who'd come up here to burn old love letters. The fire ravaged a third of the mountain before it was contained.

I felt joy at seeing so many new pines covering every square inch of the scar that had been here before. When I stood up, a head taller than them all, I felt impatient at how slow-going recovery was.

I stepped off the path to follow a stream down to a logjam. Snowmelt rushed through the rocks and formed icicles in the tangled branches. I stripped down and got in the water, shrieking with joy at the cold sting on my thighs and belly and breasts. I tilted my head back to soak my hair in the icy water.

I walked naked out on a rock shelf in the sun, and I could see the entire landscape laid out before me. A steep hillside below would take me down to the confluence of two streams, where the next day I would follow the fork of the canyon out east.

In the first few hours of the hike, I'd checked my map three times, even though I'd memorized it and knew there were no other trails to get turned around on. But now I could see it all: up the ridge to the high spot I'd come from and down into the bowl formed between the peaks around me. I didn't check the map again for the rest of the day, or the day after that.

I was done looking outside of myself for the trust and love I needed to discover within.

I'd gathered lovers around me to help me feel loved, until I realized nothing on the outside could touch what was twisting my insides. Now that I'd let them go, now that I'd stopped looking outside myself for the love I needed, I realized it was here for me: in my skin that tingled with the cold to remind me I was alive, in the little sore bones of my feet that had carried me all the places I wanted to go.

My hip flexors ached as soon as I sat down; I should have brought hiking poles. I knew I'd be wrecked the next day. No matter. That's the consequence of barreling into life like I'll never see it again.

A little worrying voice in my head said, *Why do you never think these things through?*

In my mind I saw the face of my inner wisdom. She smirked with her red fox face. *I'll die if you don't take us somewhere beautiful.*

Acknowledgments

When I'd finished the first workable draft of this book, I put a completely inappropriate level of pressure on my friend Lauren by phoning her and saying, "I need you to read this and help me assess whether it's worth the risk of putting it out there. I'm feeling incredibly vulnerable about sharing this story, but I'm willing to do it if you think it could help people."

I'd set out to write this story just for me, to make sense of myself. I honestly wanted Lauren to tell me that my convoluted, rambling manuscript about multiple relationships was too specific to really connect with many people. It would be so easy to believe that, scrap the whole thing, and never worry about getting so very naked in public.

Four hours after I sent her the draft, she texted me to say she'd just finished it and she was crying. My story had helped uncover some feelings she was going through in her own life at the time. And because I'd had the same thing happen to me reading other people's memoirs, I decided to publish this thing. If you were helped by it, you have Lauren to thank. If you hated it, now you know who to blame.

This book looked very different before Tucker Max got his hands on it. The draft I gave him had so many disconnected stories, way more anxious rambling, almost zero self-compassion and—as a result—a lot less truth. Tucker, I can't thank you enough for your time, energy, and talents, and above all, your kindness as you helped me anchor in this story.

Many thanks go to everyone at Scribe Media—it's so amazing to create books with this rad group of people, and I've been grateful for all the gorgeous work you've each poured into mine.

Special thanks to Libby, Jenn, Justine, and Juliane for reading early drafts of this book with love.

Thank you to my family, who cheered me on in creating this book even though I asked them never to read it because of how much sex is in it.

Most especially, thank you to the real-life Jordan. Sitting down to write the truth forced me to confront how much of the truth I used to avoid, and Jordan was there to accept me—and my personal truth—all the same. Your acceptance helped me throughout the whole wild experiment that appears in this book, as well as the journey of publishing it. Here's to more experiments to come.